Game-Songs
WITH PROF DOGG'S TROUPE

44 songs and games with activities
chosen by Harriet Powell
with drawings by David McKee

A & C BLACK · LONDON

Published in association with Inter-Action Inprint

Contents

Published in 1983 by A & C Black (Publishers) Ltd
35 Bedford Row London WC1R 4JH
© 1983 A & C Black (Publishers) Ltd
Reprinted 1985, 1991, 1994 and 1996

All rights reserved. No part of this publication may be reproduced or used in any form or by any means – photographic, electronic or mechanical, including photocopying, recording, taping or information storage and retrieval systems – without permission of the publishers.

ISBN 0 7136 2306 3

A CASSETTE is also available

(ISBN 0 7136 2330 6)

Printed in Great Britain by Caligraving Ltd, Thetford, Norfolk

This book was originally published in a different form by Inter-Action Inprint in the *Community Arts Series*. Editor – ED Berman.

Inter-Action is a community arts and educational charity which also offers training for those working with children and young people. *Prof Dogg's Troupe* of Inter-Action is available to perform in schools, community centres, homes and in playgrounds. For information contact:

The Administrator
Prof Dogg's Troupe of Inter-Action
HMS President (1918)
Victoria Embankment
nr Blackfriars Bridge
London EC4Y 0HJ
Tel: 0171 583 2652
FAX: 0171 583 2840

Learning Through Fun
How to use the book
Guitar chords

Gathering together

1 **Say hello**
A ritual song for saying hello. It can also include actions and acting-out.

2 **How do you do?**
A ritual meeting and greeting song

3 **Bash and Bang Band**
A parading song. Sing it as you play real or home-made instruments.

4 *Bandleader*
A rhythm game to play in a circle

5 **We're going to make a circus**
A gathering together or parading song. Use it to gather children together for any project.

Acting out

6 **Come to the party**
Acting-out things you can do at a party – or the seaside, or . . .

7 *Musicless chairs*
An acting-out game in a circle

8 **Make a face**
Make it as happy or as silly or as scary as you can!

9 *Keep your face straight*
A game to play in pairs trying to make each other laugh

10 **When a dinosaur's feeling hungry**
A song about food – what you like and where to find it

11 *Yummy corners*
A running around game with a food theme

12 **Creep up**
– but don't wake the sleeping man

13 *Burglar*
A game for moving silently and listening hard

14 **Act in song**
Be a giraffe or a mouse or anything you like in this song with a framework for including your own ideas for acting-out

15 *Knee boxing*
16 *Finger sword fighting*
Two physical games to play in pairs

17 **Be a clown**
Anything a clown can do you can do too

18 **Walking through the jungle**
– what might you see, and what would you do?

19 *Body patterns*
A game for making the shape of an animal together with your bodies

20 *Magic statues*
A follow-my-leader game in which children freeze into different shapes

Counting, colouring, clapping...

21 **Crying song**
A short song to comfort a crying child

22 **Rhyming name song**
Instant rhyme making

23 *Clap clap game*
A rhythm and word game

24 **Dice song**
Roll the dice and count the dots as you sing the song

25 **Colour song**
A song for learning about colours and how to mix them

26 *Colour collecting*
A running around game for learning colours

Actions and dances

27 **Keep on dancing**
A cumulative action song and dance

28 **Bendy toy**
An action song for bending and stretching into different shapes

29 *Clay modelling*
A game for children to move each other's bodies into different shapes

30 **Make a cake**
An action song about food, which can be turned into a spooky spell-making song

31 **Monster stomp**
Make yourself into a monster and join *The Grunt Growl Chorus*

32 **One two three**
An action song and dance in a circle

33 **I've got a body**
A cumulative action song about different parts of the body

34 *Drawing faces*
A game like consequences

35 **Mistletoe**
A Christmas action song about giving kisses

36 **We can do anything**
Challenge each other to copy your actions

37 *Ape*
A copying game to play in a circle

Actions and sounds

38 **Weather song**
A song to make the weather do what it's told

39 *Sound song*
A quiet song, listening out for sounds around you

40 *Storytelling*
Make up a story and provide the sound effects as you go along

41 **Down on the farm**
A cumulative sound and action song about farmyard animals

42 **On Christmas Day**
What would you like for Christmas and what sound would it make?

43 *Cumulative words*
A memory game about Christmas presents

44 **Say goodbye**
Sh sh sh

How the game-songs were developed
Acknowledgements
Index of titles and first lines

Game titles are given in italics

Learning Through Fun

Professor Dogg's Troupe of Inter-Action began when a few actors joined me to create a participatory play for children on the streets and playgrounds of North London. The play used colourful costumes, a conflict in the plot which the children could help resolve, a guitar or accordion, and simple songs with easy-to-pick-up tunes and words.

The plot was resolved by the children participating through games which helped move the storyline along. Out of this came the formation of the Troupe as a theatre company which created its own material for shows, projects and events in which children could take part immediately and actively especially through games and songs.

As we developed the theory and practice of Participatory Theatre throughout the seventies, the types of song also developed. One basic type used in most of the more than 150 plays created for children by the Troupe since 1968 is the game-song. This has simple words and a catchy tune; it is structured as a type of game. There are many traditional game-songs; Professor Dogg's Troupe have created new ones for different situations.

All songs that children sing teach them physical (rhythmic) co-ordination along with social and language skills which are, of course by-products of the simple act of singing. Game-songs do this more than other types of songs because of their creative structure. They can be played around with and changed, added to or acted out.

Children naturally want to use language; and the use of language is the key to most further learning. Motivation to use language is part of creative playing and singing and the child's desire to explore. Songs as games build on these natural capacities.

They encourage children to use language and to practise it in public, as it were, by singing out loud with other children. The children neither feel they are being taught to sing nor to learn anything directly. It all happens as part of the game and it's fun.

It might be interesting to look at some of the many things which can happen when children do something as seemingly simple as singing a game-song together. They can be:

- learning to listen to others
- taking turns
- having a feeling of security in a group
- speaking up in a group
- co-operating with their peer group
- making decisions to change a word or action
- accepting that changes are permissible within a set of rules
- using their imagination both physically and verbally
- enabling leadership to emerge
- thinking up responses
- practising verbal skills and vocabulary
- developing muscular co-ordination and rhythmic ability

The list above can be summarized in three categories of skills: communication, social and language.

There is a fourth area – emotional development. When a child plays the game-song of creeping up on a sleeping man who then wakes up with a roar (*12 Creep up*), there is a potential for different kinds of emotional expression – fear, laughter and pleasure.

All of this adds up to game-songs being particularly useful in developing confidence and a range of basic skills. The nicest thing about it, when all the analysis is over, is that game-songs are simply a great deal of fun.

ED Berman MBE

How to use the book

Singing these game-songs is child's play! All the invention, energy and fun in children's play is here in a game-song too. As well as enjoying singing together, children can join in with all kinds of physical activity, from wiggling eyebrows to doing the monster stomp.

Game-songs encourage children to play inventively with the words of songs and to make up new versions. They present many opportunities for children and adults to choose their own actions, sounds and words within the basic framework of each game-song. Just like children's games they have themes of fantasy or reality or a mixture of both.

All the game-songs in the collection have been written over the last twelve years by actors and musicians associated with Inter-Action's Prof Dogg's Troupe, several of whom have also worked at Interplay Community Theatre, Leeds. All the songs have been sung with children under seven as well as children of a wider age range and some have been used with children with various disabilities.

We have used them hundreds of times in all sorts of places – parks, playgroups, schools, clubs for children with handicaps, and with our own children at home.

Types of game-songs
Alongside the heading 'basic use' we indicate the game-song's type and purpose. There are ritual songs, action songs, sound effect songs, acting-out songs, parading songs, gathering together songs, and dances. Most songs have a combination of purposes, for example actions and sound effects. Many of the songs have

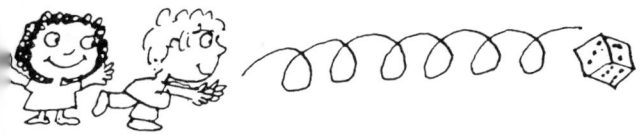

themes such as the circus, the jungle or the weather which children, like the rest of us, can easily relate to.

Most of the game-songs are constructed to allow the children's suggestions to be incorporated. For example:

— Rhymes: *Rhyming name song* needs children to provide rhymes for each others names
— Words: *Make a cake* encourages children to think of ingredients for a cake
— Words and sounds: *On Christmas Day* requires suggestions of toys the children might receive at Christmas and the sounds the toys might make
— Actions: *I've got a body* needs suggestions for what you do with different parts of your body

Basic use
Under this heading we give you guidance on how to use each game-song in its basic form.

Try this
Under this heading we list further ways of using the game-song. Introduce different ways of playing the game-songs yourself or ask children to suggest ways before singing the song. Here are some examples of how we have developed them:

— Exploring the theme further. For example, the *Weather song*, which is a song for singing about different kinds of weather, can be sung to include ideas for what you do or wear in different kinds of weather.
— Changing a theme. *Come to the party* can become *Come to the seaside*
— Changing a character. The dinosaur in *When a dinosaur's feeling hungry* can become another animal or a person
— Including actions. *Say hello* can be changed to *Clap your hands* or *Be a train*

Also under this heading we give you some ideas for extending the game-songs into other activities such as craft work or storytelling. Alternatively, an activity may lead you into an appropriate game-song. Here are some possibilities:

— after singing *Walking through the jungle* children could paint jungle pictures, or reading a jungle story might lead to singing *Walking through the jungle*
— often the song and activity can be combined. Animal costumes could be made with the children and worn while singing *Walking through the jungle*

Remember that our suggestions are only starting points. You will think of more possibilities than we have ever tried.

The music
The tunes are simple and fun to sing. Children pick them up very quickly. We have given chord symbols above each melody and a piano accompaniment to most of the songs for those who want to use an instrument to accompany the singing.

The tape
This has been recorded to help both those who don't read music and those who do. Listening and singing along will enable you to learn the tunes and feel confident singing them with children even without accompaniment. Even if you do read music, you may like to listen to the tape with the children and get to know the song together.

The recordings differ from the book in that we have made up new words in those songs which are meant to elicit suggestions from the children. We recommend that you listen to how the children's suggestions could fit in in place of ours. Then sing the songs allowing the children to introduce their own words and ideas.

The games
Alongside the songs is a collection of non-musical games in strip cartoon form. These are games which we often play before or after singing a song. Most of them connect with a theme in the game-song they accompany. For instance the actions in a song may lead into a non-musical game or vice versa:

— *Bendy toy* can lead to the game called *Clay modelling* in which children bend each other into shapes.

Here is one more game. Try making up your own game-song using a well-known tune as we have done with *Rhyming name song*. We have found the habit of playing around with songs a creative one – we hope you will too.

Harriet Powell

Guitar chords

A 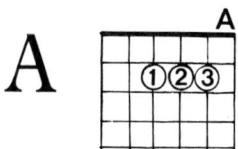 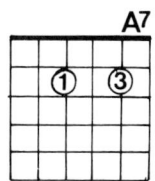 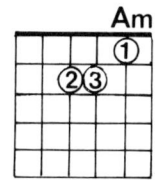 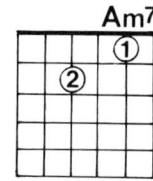   E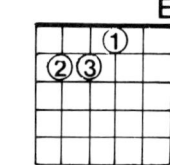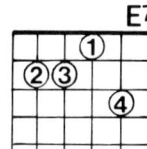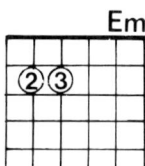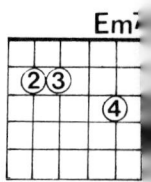

B♭    B 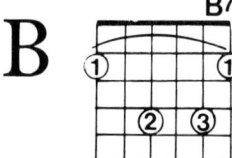 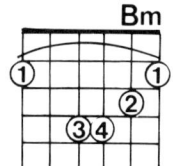   F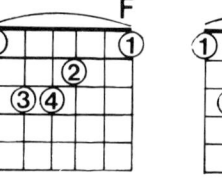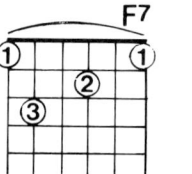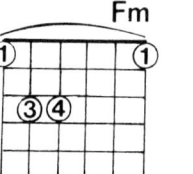

C 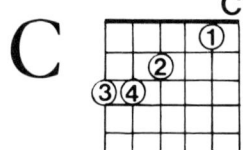 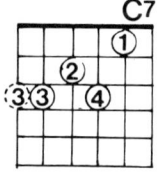 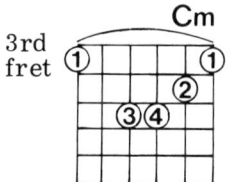   G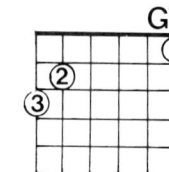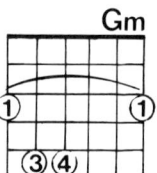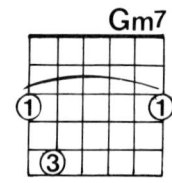

D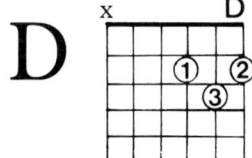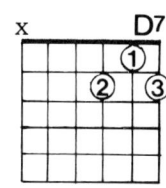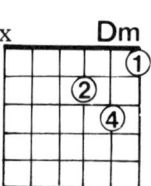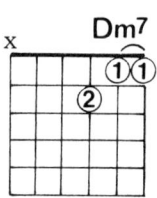

x   silent string

   barré: press all strings down with first finger

Say hello

Maggie Anwell, Tony Coult, John Rust and Charlie Stafford

Leader	Children
Say hello	Hello
Say hello	Hello
Say hello	Hello
Say hello	Hello

Basic use – a ritual song for saying hello

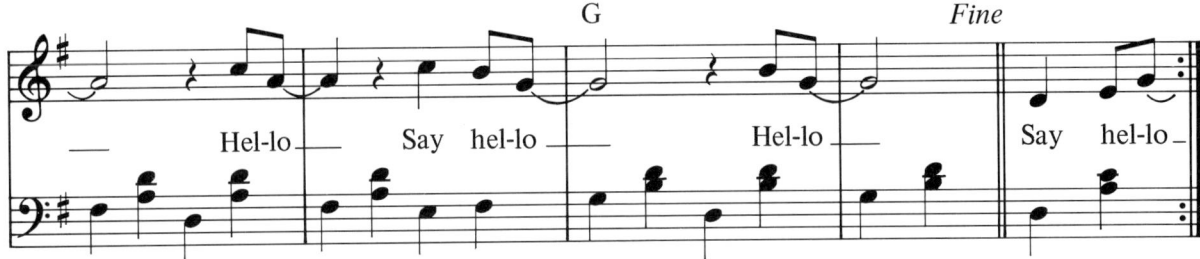

Try this

☆ Say hello to a different child each time. You don't need to repeat all four lines for each name – one or two would do:

Hello John___ Hello John
Hello John___ Hello John
Hello Pete___ Hello Pete . . .

☆ Fit in words describing actions. The leader can sing the action and perform it, encouraging the children to copy:

Clap your hands___ *clap clap clap*
Clap your hands___ *clap clap clap*

☆ Pretend to be something or someone else. The children can act out the movements and imitate the sound of whatever the leader tells them to be:

Be a train___ *chuff chuff chuff*
Be a train___ *chuff chuff chuff*

☆ Turn the song into a game. Ask the children to do and/or sing the opposite of the instruction. For example:

Leader	Children
Say hello	Goodbye
All sit down	All stand up . . .

2 How do you do?

ED Berman

How do you do?
How do you do?
I'm very pleased to meet you,
I'm very pleased to meet you,
How do you do?
How do you do?

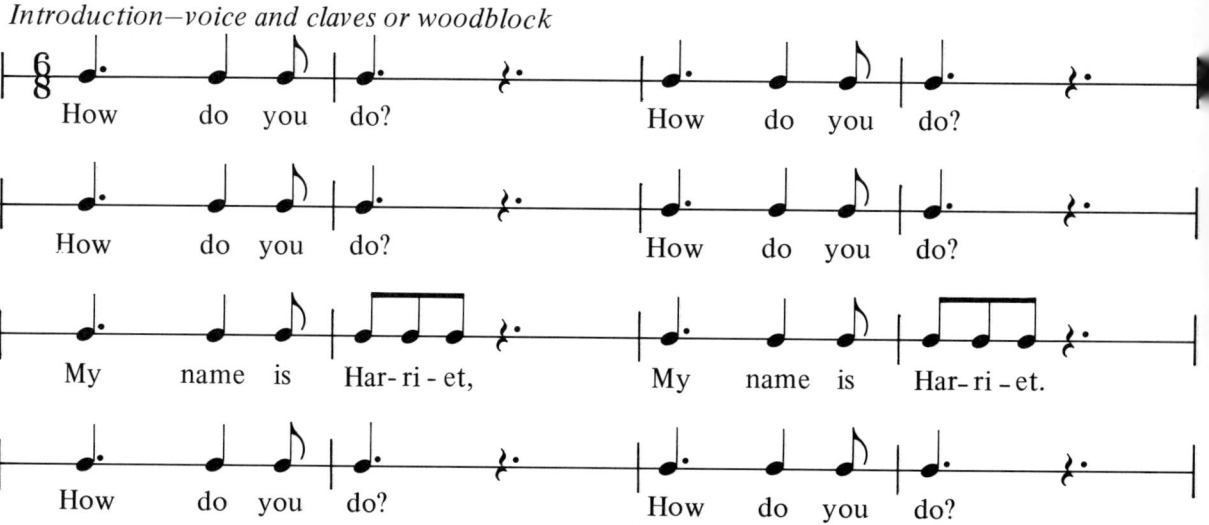

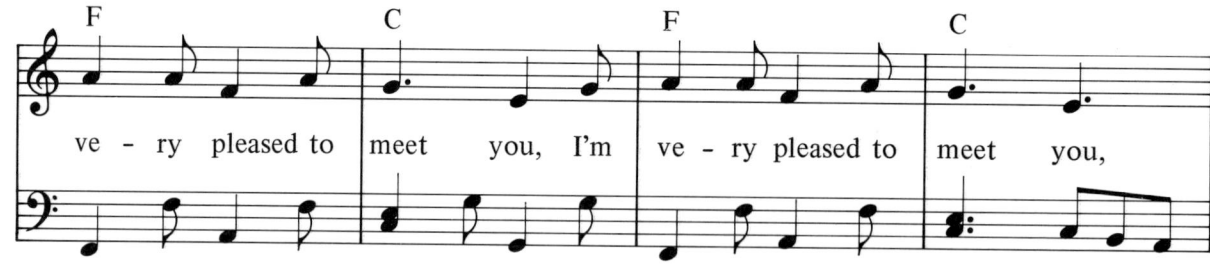

Basic use – a ritual meeting and greeting song

Young children pick this song up very quickly. The leader may like to accentuate the rhythm by accompanying the singing on a percussion instrument. You can play the melody rhythm, a steady pulse of dotted crochet beats (first rhythm given below), or play the rhythm of the words "how do you do" throughout:

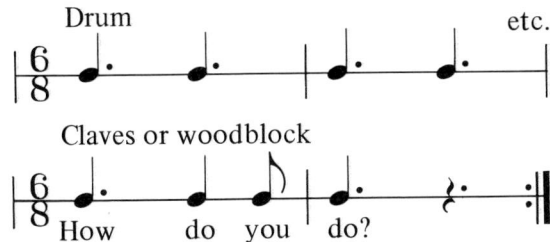

Introduce the song to the children by rhythmically chanting the words "how do you do" over and over, then introducing your own name (see the Introduction).

Try this

☆ Get all the children shaking hands with each other by singing the first two bars of the melody to these words (the rhythm needs to be altered slightly):

Everyone hold hands
Everyone hold hands
Shake them up and down
Shake them up and down

Now we can sing
Now we can sing

Then start the song again at "how do you do". Encourage the children to fit in other actions, such as clapping to the rhythm, in the same way.

3 Bash and Bang Band

Ian Heywood

We are the Circus Bash and Bang Band
Bash bash bash, kicking up a din.
We are the Circus Bash and Bang Band
Bang bang bang, everyone join in.
    La la
    La la la lala la la
    Lala la la la la
    (Repeat)

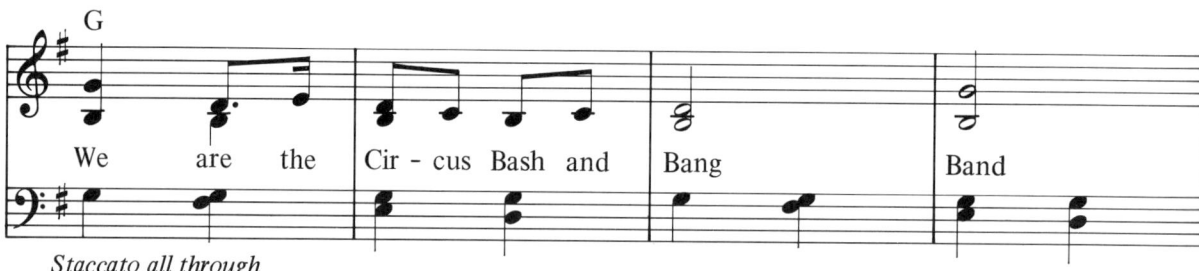

Staccato all through

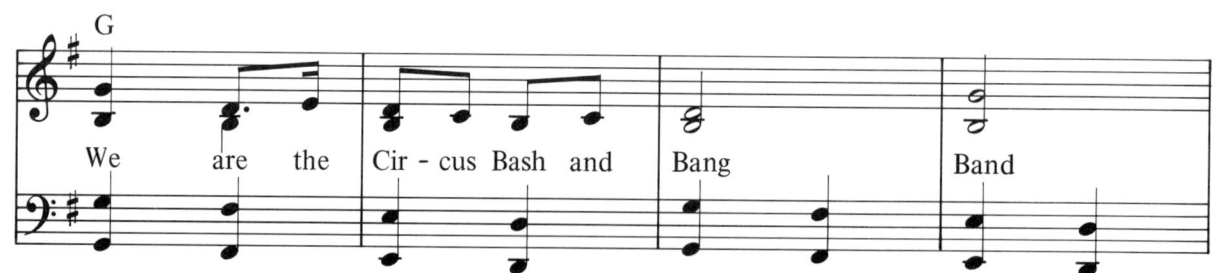

4 Bandleader

Bang bang bang, eve-ry-one join in. La la La la la la- la la la La- la la la la la (La la)

To develop the game...

Basic use – a parading song

A song which children can accompany with home-made instruments. The name *Circus Bash and Bang Band* is used as an example and you can insert any name you like for your band, e.g. the name of your school or playgroup.

Try this

☆ Make your own instruments – plastic bottle maracas, tin can drums, pan lid cymbals – then sing the song and parade round using your instruments to play along on "bash bash bash", "bang bang bang" and in the "la la" section.

☆ If you don't have instruments, imitate the sounds instead, e.g. drum (boom boom boom) or trumpet (toot toot toot). This will work well in the "la la" section where everyone can make the sound of their instrument and mime playing it instead of singing to la.

☆ Call out one type of instrument to be played or mimed during the "la la" section while the others keep silent.

5 We're going to make a circus

Leon Rosselson

We're going to make a circus
We're going to make a circus
We're going to make a circus
The greatest show on earth.

Leader	*Children*
It's gigantic	It's gigantic
It'll be frantic	It'll be frantic
Thrill a minute	Thrill a minute
Come along and be in it	Come along and be in it

Basic use – gathering together or parading

All sing the first section together, then in the second section the children sing the repeated line after the leader. Each section can be repeated as many times as you like. You can use the song as a means of gathering a group of children together for a project. Change the words to suit the situation, e.g. "We're going to paint a picture"

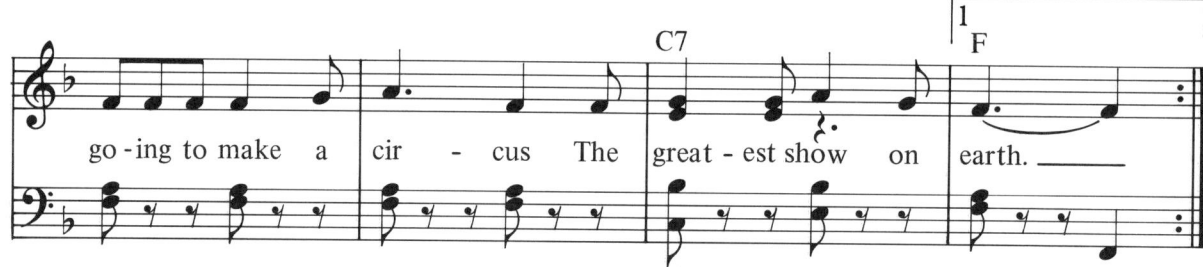

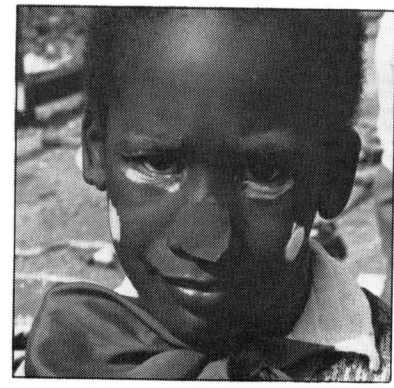

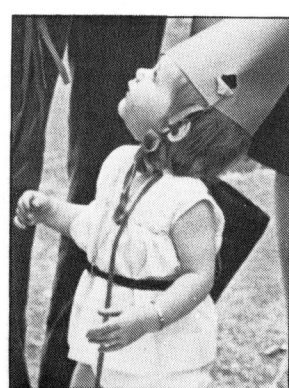

Try this

☆ Have a face painting session choosing a number of different characters to paint yourselves as. All sit in a circle then ask one of your characters or a group of them to dance, crawl, growl, or whatever is appropriate, in the middle of the circle. Meanwhile the other children can sing the first section of the song with suitable new words, e.g.

> We can see a tiger
> We can see a tiger
> We can see a tiger
> The wildest tiger on earth.

☆ Make a circus: spend a day helping the children prepare for and perform their own circus. Make costumes and props from junk materials and rehearse the acts the children want to perform. When you are ready, gather a circle of friends, parents and neighbours and put on a performance.

6 Come to the party

George Dewey

Come to the party come to the party
Come to the party come right now,
Think of something you want to do
And you can do it right now.

You can eat cake on your own
You can eat cake with a friend
You can eat cake with everybody
And you can do it right now.
    Come to the party . . .

You can have a dance on your own
You can have a dance with a friend
You can have a dance with everybody
And you can do it right now.
    Come to the party . . .

You can . . . on your own . . .

Basic use – an acting-out song

After singing the chorus together, get suggestions from children for different things you can do at a party and act them out while singing each new verse.

You can eat cake with eve-ry-bo-dy And you can do it right now.

Try this

☆ Replace party with any different theme. For example:

Come to the seaside come to the seaside
Come to the seaside come right now,
Think of something you want to do
And you can do it right now.
   Ask "What can you do at the seaside?"

You can have a paddle on your own
You can have a paddle with a friend
You can have a paddle with everybody
And you can do it right now.
   Come to the seaside . . .
   Ask again

You can . . . on you own . . .

☆ Use as a gathering together or parading song after an activity such as face painting, dressing up, or mask making. Alter the theme to whatever is appropriate – circus, farmyard, pantomime.

7 Musicless chairs

Change the theme to whatever you like, e.g. shepherds, sheep and sheep-dogs.

8 Make a face

George Dewe

If you want to be happy
And have a happy day,
And spread a bit of joy around
Then there is just one way:

Make a face
Make a face
Make it as happy as you can
And make a face.
    If you want to be happy . . .

Make a face
Make a face
Make it as scary as you can
And make a face.
    If you want to be happy . . .

Make a face
Make a face
Make it as silly as you can
And make a face.
    If you want to be happy . . .

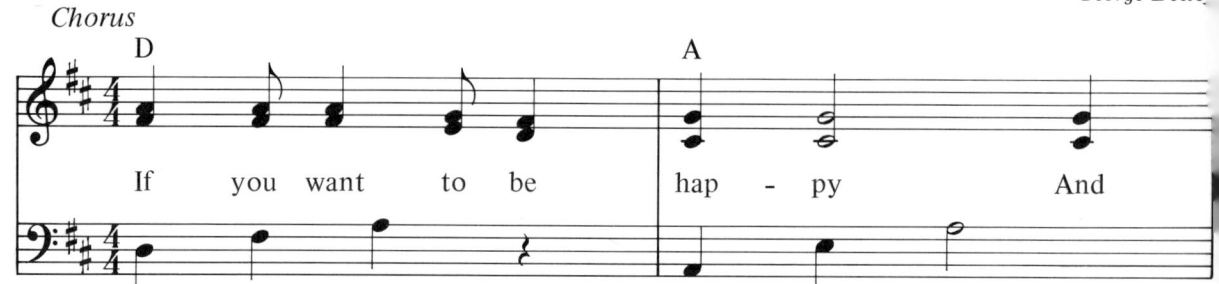
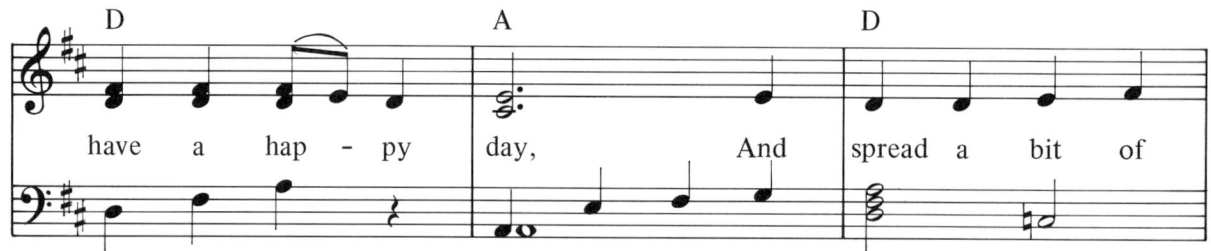

Basic use – an acting-out song

After singing the chorus together ask the children what sort of faces they can make – happy, silly, angry. Choose one and repeat the verse or chorus as many times as you like while you all make that face. Sing the chorus again then start a new verse.

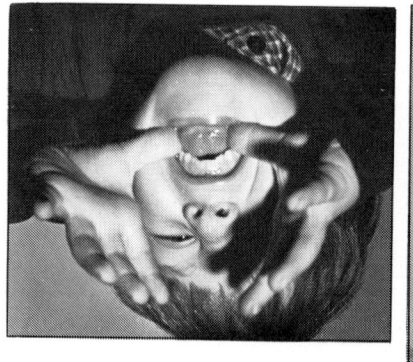
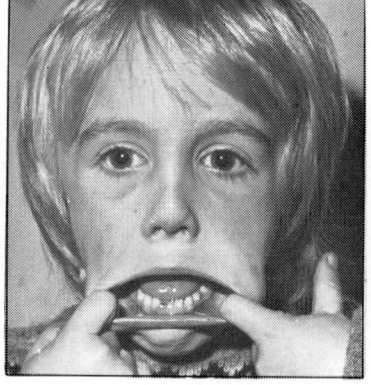
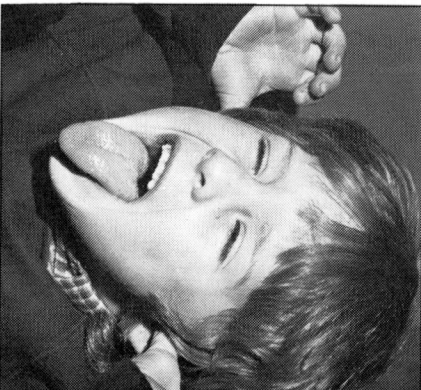

9 Keep your face straight

Ask: "What sort of face can you make?" then sing...

Verse

Make a face — Make a face —

Sing through the verse or chorus as often as you like while you all make happy faces

Make it as hap-py as you can And make a face. —

Try this

☆ Substitute statues for faces and ask the children what sort of statue they would like to make, e.g.

Make a statue
Make a statue
As much like a monster as you can
And make a statue.

☆ Make a sound: ask the children in turn to think of a funny, imaginative, quiet, or loud sound on different instruments or using their voices, e.g.

Make a sound
Make a sound
Make it as quiet as you can
And make a sound.

1. Everyone chooses a partner

2. One child makes a face and must keep the expression fixed

3. His partner must try to make him laugh or change his face without touching him.

10 When a dinosaur's feeling hungry

Charlie Stafford and the children of Quarry Hill Flats, Leeds

When a dinosaur's feeling hungry
He looks for food.
He looks in the forest
When he's in a hungry mood.
When he looks in the forest
He finds lots and lots of trees,
When he looks in the forest
He finds lots and lots of mice.
    And he goes mmm – trees
    And he goes ugh – mice
    And he goes mmm – trees
    And he goes ugh – mice.
    When a dinosaur's feeling hungry
    He looks for food.

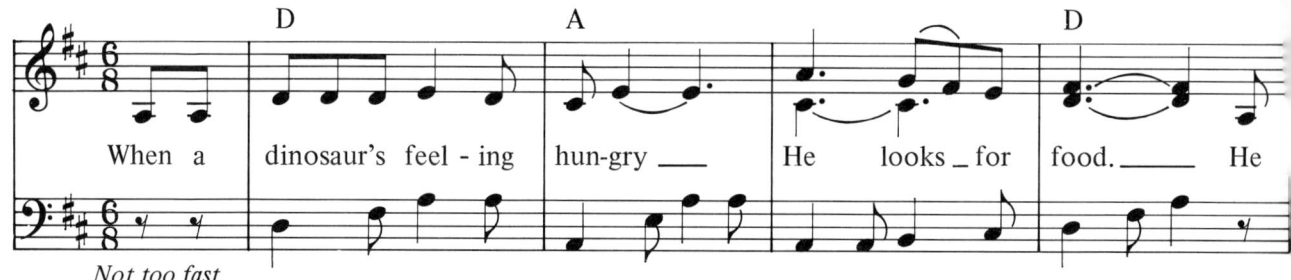

Basic use – an acting-out song

Before you start the song, ask the children where a dinosaur might look for food, and what it would and wouldn't like to eat. Fit their suggestions into the appropriate places in the song, making up as many new verses as you like.

11 Yummy corners

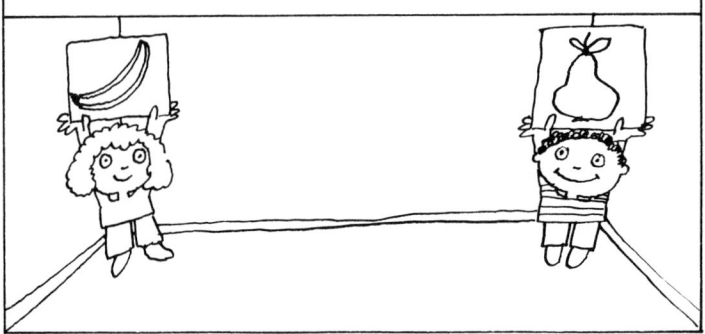

In each corner of the room a child holds a large picture of a food.

If the leader shouts 'Banana', the children must run to that corner

When they get there they can act out being the food, or the kind of animal that eats the food.

Try this

☆ Make up a new verse for each child in turn, asking them what they can and can't eat or what they do and don't like eating, and where they would go to find it:

> When Pete is feeling hungry
> He looks for food.
> He looks in the kitchen
> When he's in a hungry mood.
> When he looks in the kitchen
> He finds lots and lots of cake,
> When he looks in the kitchen
> He finds lots and lots of soap.
>   And he goes mmm – cake
>   And he goes ugh – soap . . .

☆ Instead of a dinosaur, think of another character to sing about – human, animal, or otherwise. You might choose a character from a favourite story. As you sing the song you could all move round the room pretending to be the person you are singing about. Ask the children what they can find in the room which your new character would and wouldn't like eating. Fit their suggestions into the song to make new verses.

☆ Put some edible things like different pieces of fruit into one bag, and into another bag put some inedible objects – a piece of string, soap, rubber. As you sing the song, a child can pick one thing from each bag with which to complete the lines of the verse.

12 Creep up

Keith Erskin[e]

Sam creep up, creep up
As quietly as you can.
Sam creep up, creep up
Don't wake the sleeping man.

Sam pat the pig on the head – *pat pat pat*
Sam pat the pig on the back – *pat pat pat*
Sam pat the pig on the head – *pat pat pat*
Oh oh oh oh I say,
You'd better run away!

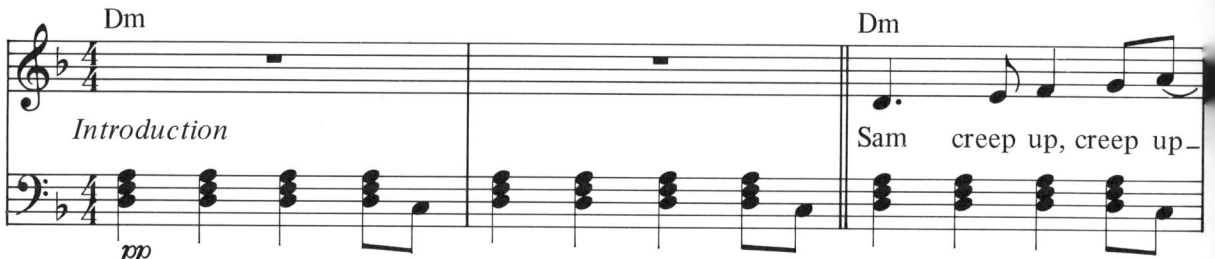
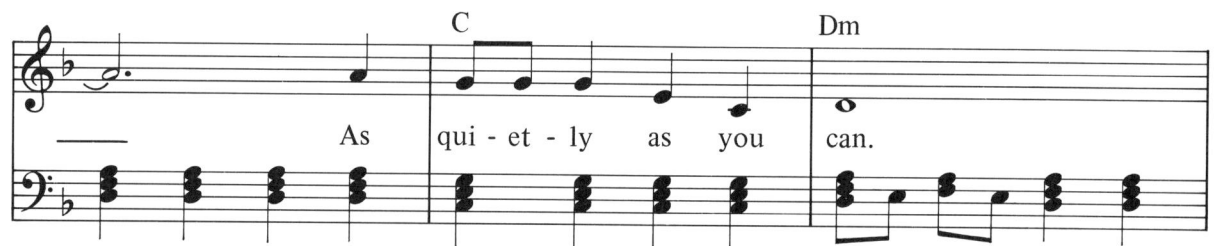

Basic use – an acting-out song

Each child in turn creeps up to a sleeping character (in our example a farmer with a pig). Another child can be this character. The child creeping up is trying to steal the pig from the farmer. After the third time of patting the pig, the farmer wakes up with a loud yawn or roar, and the child runs away.

13 Burglar

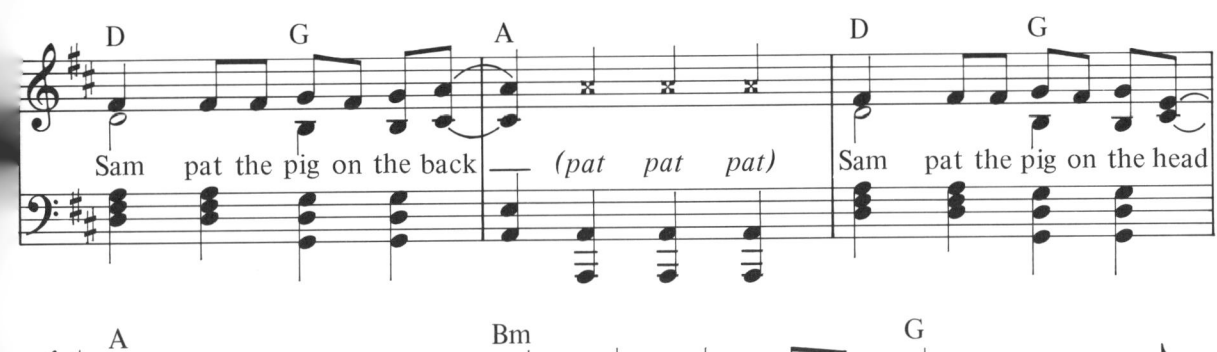

1. Blindfold one child who will guard an object in the middle of the circle without touching it.

2. A burglar is chosen who has to creep into the circle to take the object.

3. The guard listens and tries to catch the burglar.

4. If the burglar takes the object without being caught the guard must guess who the burglar was.

Try this

☆ Hide someone in a large cardboard box or basket and give them a collection of loud sound makers – whistle, football rattle, hooter. The other children creep up in turn and knock the basket. After the third time the person inside makes one of the loud sounds:

Maggie creep up, creep up
As quietly as can be
Maggie creep up, creep up
I wonder what we'll see.

Maggie give the basket a knock – *knock knock knock*
Careful or you might get a shock – *knock knock knock*
Maggie give the basket a knock – *knock knock knock*
Oh oh oh oh I say,
You'd better run away!

14 Act in song

ED Berman

La la lala la la
Lala la la la lalala la
La la lala la la
Lala la la la lalala la

Standing up, standing up
Everybody standing up.
Standing up, standing up
Everybody standing up.
  La la lala la la . . .

Basic use – an action and acting-out song

Any number of suggestions for verses can be fitted into the format of this song – "standing up" is simply given as an example. Sing the chorus then repeat the verse with its actions as many times as you like.

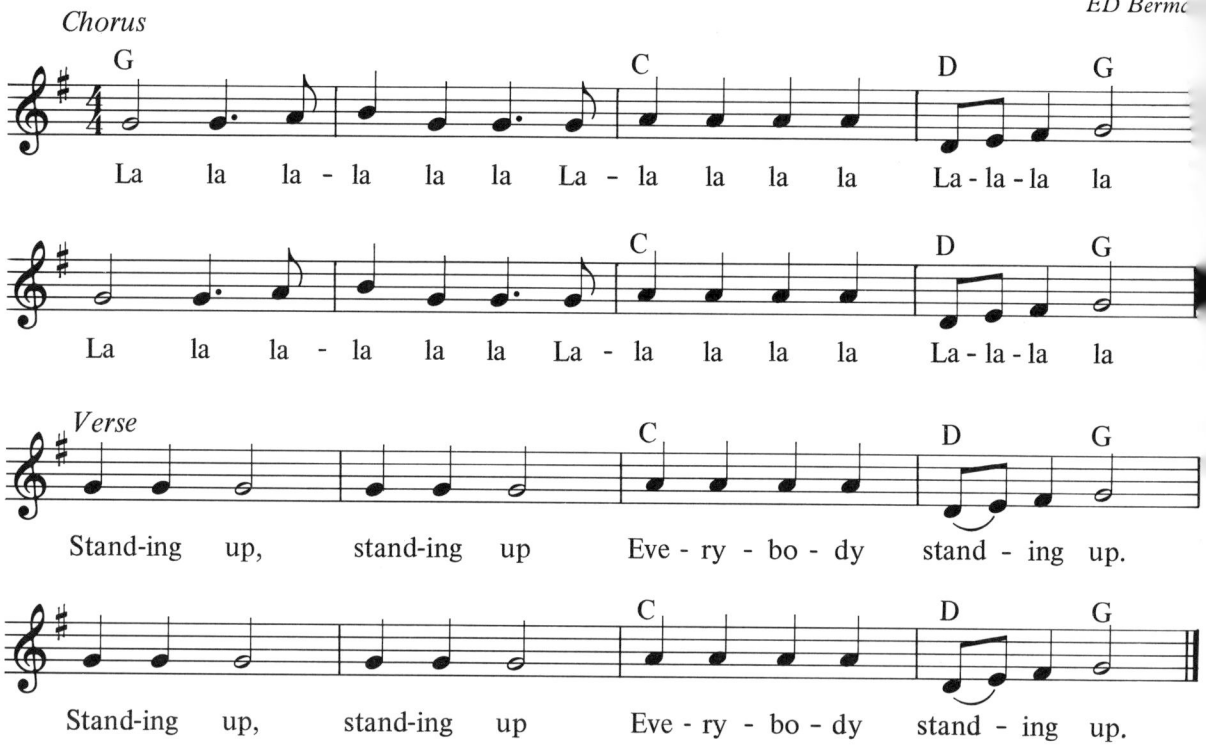

Try this

☆ To form a circle sing:

In a circle, in a circle
In a circle, round we go.
In a circle, in a circle
In a circle, round we go.

☆ Act out different characters:

Be a giraffe, be a giraffe
Stretch up tall just like a giraffe.
(Repeat)

Be a mouse, be a mouse
Curl up small just like a mouse,
(Repeat)

Be a . . .

15 Knee boxing

1) Everyone choose a partner

2) Stand opposite your partner and put your hands on your knees

3) Try and touch your partner's knees without letting him touch yours.

4) Development: leave partner and try to touch anybody's knees.

16 Finger sword fighting

1) Everyone choose a partner

2) Put one hand behind your back and point your finger at your partner. Your finger is your sword

3) See if you can touch your partner's back without letting your partner touch yours.

4) Leave partner and try to touch anybody's back

17 Be a clown

Harriet Powe

Be a clown, be a clown
Some are big and some are small,
They can do anything at all
Be a clown, be a clown.

A clown can pull a funny face
You can pull a funny face
You can pull a funny face too,
A clown can pull a funny face
You can pull a funny face
You can pull a funny face too.
    Be a clown . . .

A clown can jump up and down
You can jump up and down
You can jump up and down too . . .
    Be a clown . . .

A clown can . . .

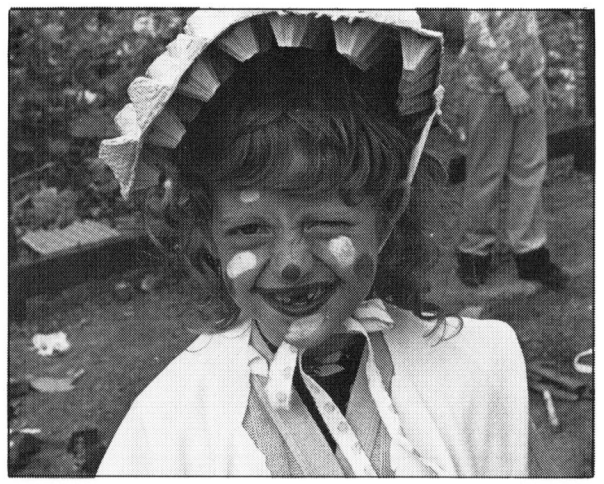

Basic use – an acting-out song

During the chorus, dance around like clowns. Take suggestions from the children for things a clown can do and act these out in each new verse. You might use the song after a face painting session or as part of the circus project suggested in 5 *We're going to make a circus*.

Try this

☆ Instead of being clowns choose another character to sing about and imitate, making up a new verse each time as above, or thinking of a new character at each new chorus:

> Be a frog, be a frog
> Some are big and some are small,
> They can do anything at all
> Be a frog, be a frog.
>
> A frog can hop along the ground
> You can hop along the ground
> You can hop along the ground too . . .
>   *Repeat*
>   Be a frog . . .
>
> Be a bird, be a bird . . .
>
> A bird can flap its wings about
> You can flap your wings about
> You can flap your wings about too . . .
>   *Repeat*
>   Be a bird . . .

18 Walking through the jungle

Harriet Power

Walking through the jungle, walking through
   the jungle,
What do you see? What do you see?
If you hear a noise – sh – sh – sh –
What could it be? What could it be?

Oh well I think it was a snake – *hiss*
Think it was a snake – *hiss*
Think it was a snake – *hiss*
Looking for his tea, looking for his tea.
   (Repeat)
      Walking through the jungle . . .

Basic use – an acting-out song

The children can sing the repeated lines in the chorus after the leader, or everyone can sing all the lines together. Sing as you walk round the room pretending to be explorers. If you sing it sitting down, pat your knees in rhythm during the chorus. At the end of the chorus get a child to make an animal noise, then sing the verse, joining in with appropriate noises and actions.

Try this

☆ Try different themes – *Walking through the countryside* or *Walking down the high street*.

☆ Change the words so that you sing about what you would do if you saw an animal in the jungle. Ask the children for suggestions for the animal and what they would do to get away from it. For example if they saw a tiger then they might sing the verse given opposite.

19 Body patterns

Walking through the jungle, walking through the jungle,
What do you see? What do you see?
If you see a tiger, if you see a tiger
Looking for his tea, looking for his tea

Then we must swing through the creepers
   (Tarzan call)
Swing through the creepers (Tarzan call)
Swing through the creepers (Tarzan call)
Then we won't be his tea, we won't be his tea.
   (Repeat)

20 Magic statues

21 Crying song

ED Berman

Tom, why are you crying?
Crying won't help you.
If you stop your crying
You will find that you can do
The things you want to do.

Basic use

You may like to sing this to any crying child.

22 Rhyming name song

Traditional melody

His name is Pete
His name is Pete
His name is Pete
And he's got great big feet.

Her name is Harriet
Her name is Harriet
Her name is Harriet
Her piano's too heavy to carry it.

Basic use

Make up a verse for each child's name and your own. Ask the children to provide the rhymes for their friends. If they are stuck for one you'll have to think of it! After singing the third line of the verse, stop and ask the children what rhymes with Pete (or whatever other name you are singing) then make up a line to finish the verse. Then sing right through the verse again without a break.

23 Clap clap game

His name is Pete — And he's got great big feet. —

Ask someone else what their name is and start again

Try this

☆ Instead of finding rhymes for names, ask each child for his or her favourite food and make up rhymes for these:

Robert likes eating jam
Robert likes eating jam
Robert likes eating jam
He eats it with some spam.

☆ Ask the children to tell you their favourite colours and make rhymes for these:

Pete likes red
Pete likes red
Pete likes red
It's the colour of his bed.

24 Dice song

Harriet Powe

We've got one dot on top of the dice,
Roll it over again.
When it stops we'll count the dots,
Roll it over again.

How many dots have we got now?
Count together and see –
1 – 2 – 3
We've got three dots on top of the dice,
Roll it over again.
    We've got three dots . . .

How many dots have we got now?
Count together and see –
1 – 2 – 3 – 4 – 5 – 6
We've got six dots on top of the dice,
Roll it over again.
    We've got six dots . . .

Basic use – a counting game

Make or buy a large dice. Start the chorus by singing whichever number happens to be on top. Each child then has a turn to roll the dice during the chorus. In the pause in the verse all count together how many dots have landed on top.

Try this

☆ Before you sing the song, choose an action for each of the numbers on the dice. For example, if it lands on 1, jump once; on 2, wave two hands; on 3, hop three times, etc. Either the child who rolled the dice has to remember to do the action during the pause in the verse, or all the children can do it together:

> How many dots have we got now?
> Do this action and see –

> We've got three hops on top of the dice,
> Roll it over again.
>   We've got three hops . . .

25 Colour song

George Dew

Take a little bit of yellow
And a little bit of blue,
Put it in a bowl and mix it up do,
We've got a colour we've never had before,
What have we got? We've got green.
    We can mix lots of colours
    All the colours you've ever seen,
    We can mix lots of colours
    Yellow and blue make green.

Take a little bit of yellow
And a little bit of red,
Put it in a bowl and what have you got instead?
We've got a colour we've never had before,
What have we got? We've got orange.
    We can mix lots of colours
    All the colours you've ever seen,
    We can mix lots of colours
    Yellow and red make orange,
    And yellow and blue make green.

Take a little bit of red
And a little bit of blue,
Put it in a bowl and mix it up do,
We've got a colour we've never had before,
What have we got? We've got purple.
    We can mix lots of colours
    All the colours you've ever seen,
    We can mix lots of colours
    Red and blue make purple,
    Yellow and red make orange,
    And yellow and blue make green.

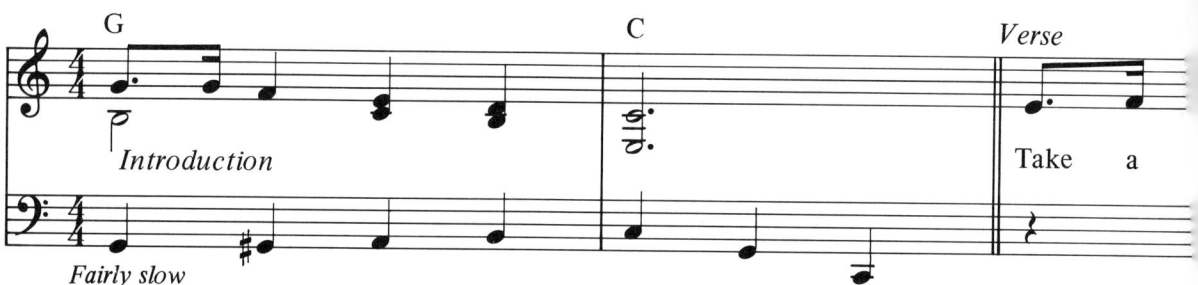

26 Colour collecting

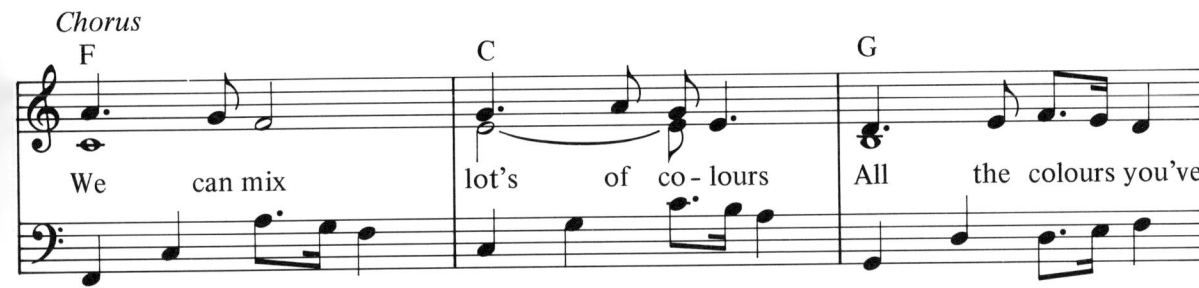

ne-ver had be-fore, What have we got? We've got green.

Chorus

We can mix lot's of co-lours All the colours you've e-ver seen, We can mix lots of co-lours

Second and third time only

Yel-low and red make orange, _____ And yel-low and blue make green.

27 Keep on dancing

Judy Farrar, Janice Honeyman, Katina Noble and Harriet Powell

Keep on dancing, keep on dancing
Keep on singing this song.
Keep on dancing, keep on dancing
Keep on singing this song.

Clap your hands and stamp your feet
Wiggle your eyebrows to the beat,
Wiggle your eyebrows, wiggle your eyebrows,
Keep on singing this song.
    Keep on dancing . . .

Clap your hands and stamp your feet
Shake your shoulders to the beat,
Shake your shoulders, shake your shoulders,
Wiggle your eyebrows, wiggle your eyebrows,
Keep on singing this song.
    Keep on dancing . . .

Clap your hands and stamp your feet
Knobble your kneecaps to the beat,
Knobble your kneecaps, knobble your kneecaps,
Shake your shoulders, shake your shoulders,
Wiggle your eyebrows, wiggle your eyebrows,
Keep on singing this song.
    Keep on dancing . . .

Clap your hands and stamp your feet
Wobble your bottom to the beat,
Wobble your bottom, wobble your bottom,
Knobble your kneecaps, knobble your kneecaps,
Shake your shoulders, shake your shoulders,
Wiggle your eyebrows, wiggle your eyebrows,
Keep on singing this song.

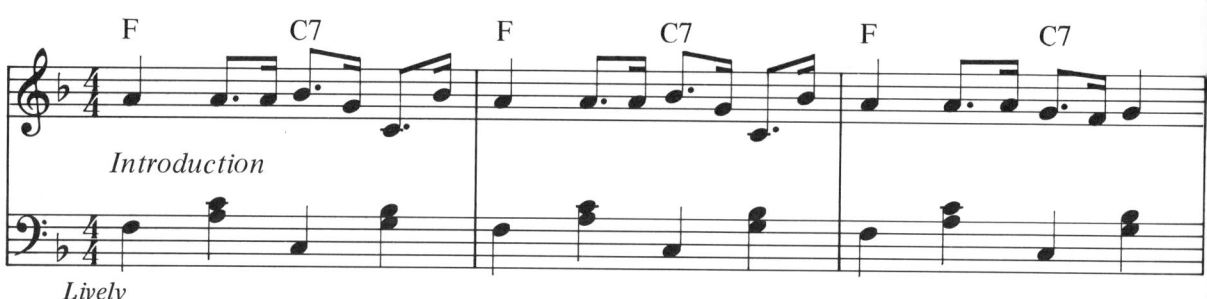

Verse

```
C                              F                    G
Clap your hands and      stamp your feet      Wig-gle your eye-brows

C                              F      C7             F      C7
to the beat,             Wig-gle your eye-brows, wig-gle your eye-brows,

F           C7           F
Keep on sing-ing this song.
```

Basic use – a cumulative action song and dance

During the chorus, dance around in a circle holding hands. At the start of the verse stop dancing and do the actions indicated instead. By the way, "knobble your kneecaps" means knock your knees together. Start by doing the actions slowly and get faster as you become more accomplished.

Try this

☆ During the chorus, dance on the spot in a group or in a circle. Choose one person's way of dancing for everyone to copy. Invent silly ones.

☆ Change the actions in the verse. Use different parts of the body and fit in different words, e.g. "wiggle your fingers".

☆ As a finale – an impossible but funny challenge – try doing all the actions at once.

> Clap your hands and stamp your feet
> Do all the actions to the beat . . .

28 Bendy toy

Harriet Power

Bendy bends to any shape
He bends and stretches, he won't break.
Try and copy the shapes he makes
And be a bendy toy.

Well, he bends over here
He bends over there
As round as a ball
Or straight as a chair,
And if you think you're a piece of elastic
You'll be looking quite fantastic!
    Bendy bends to any shape . . .

Well, he bends over here
He bends over there
As tall as a tree
Or as wide as a bear
And if you think you're a piece of elastic
You'll be looking quite fantastic!
    Bendy bends to any shape . . .

Basic use – an action song

While singing the chorus, all bend and stretch in any way you like. During the verses, the children can pretend to be bendy toys, doing all the actions indicated in the words.

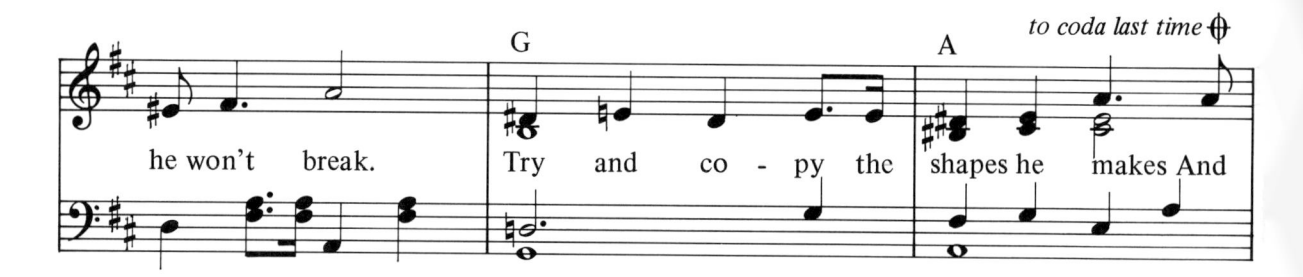

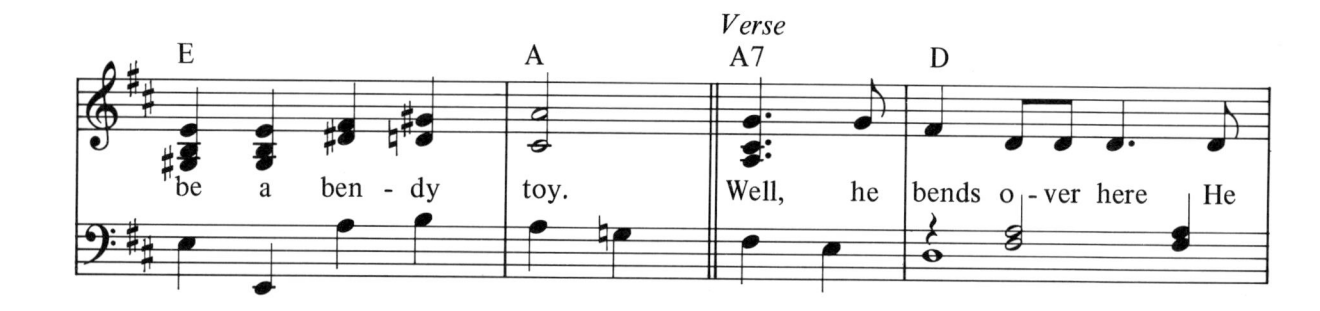

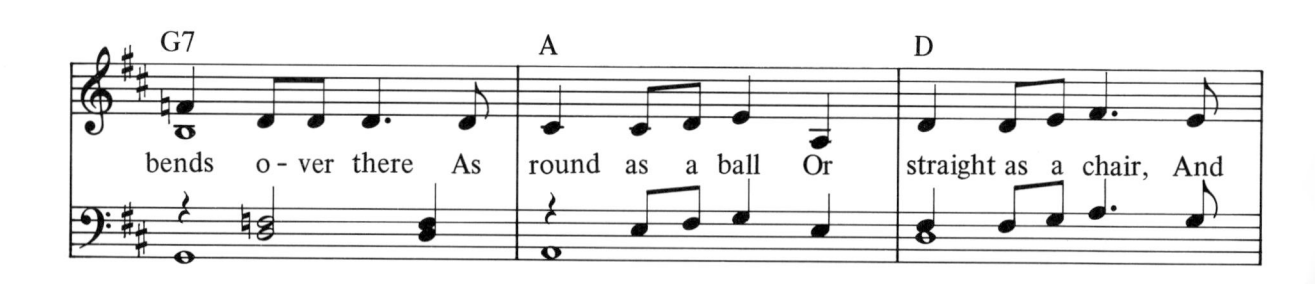

29 Clay modelling

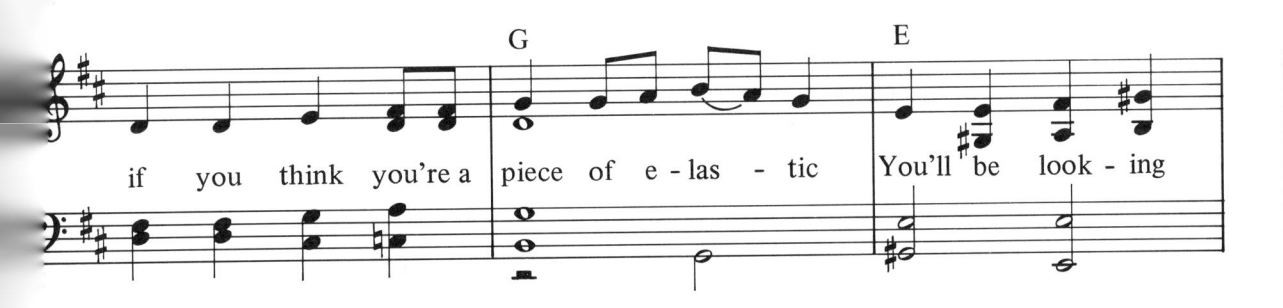

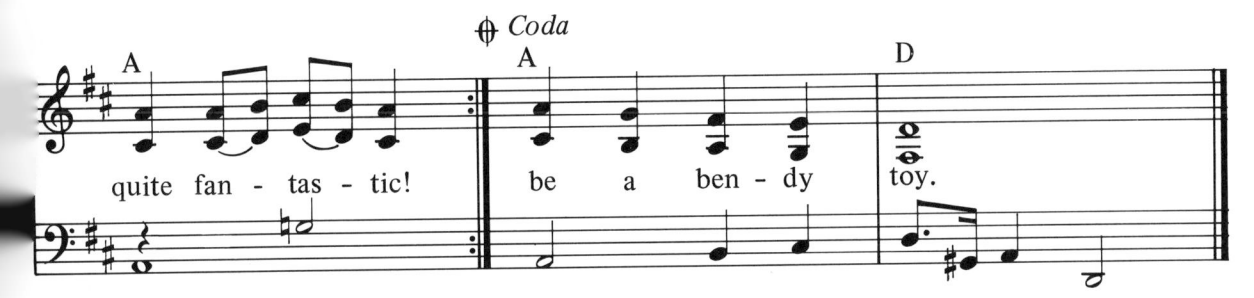

...if you think you're a piece of elastic You'll be looking quite fantastic! be a bendy toy.

Well, he bends over here 
He bends over there 
As round as a ball
Or straight as a chair

As tall as a tree 
Or as wide as a bear

Try this

☆ Change or add to the actions by making up new verses, e.g.

> He stretches up high
> He bends down low
> Nods his head "yes"
> Shakes it "no".

1 A child stands in the middle and pretends to be a lump of clay

2 The leader models the lump of clay into a shape

3 Leader chooses a child in the circle to change the shape

4 New people can be added.

30 Make a cake

Harriet Power

Let's make a cake
Let's make a cake
Mix in all the things that we like best,
A little bit of this,
A little bit of that,
What shall we put in first?

And we shall mix in the eggs
Mix in the eggs
Stir and stir and
Stir and stir and
    Let's make a cake . . .
    (In the last line sing
    next instead of first)

And we shall mix in the icecream
Mix in the icecream
Stir and stir and
Stir and stir and
    Let's make a cake . . .

And we shall mix in the . . .

Basic use – an action song

Make stirring actions as you sing. At the words "a little bit of this, a little bit of that" pretend to put things into the bowl. At "what shall we put in first/next?" take suggestions from the children for what to mix in the cake. It doesn't matter how unlikely an ingredient it is.

Try this

☆ Use a different theme such as witches and wizards mixing spells. Revolting suggestions for ingredients are guaranteed! This is especially appropriate for Halloween:

> Let's make a spell
> Let's make a spell
> Put in all the things to make it work,
> A little bit of this
> A little bit of that,
> What shall we put in first?
>
> And we will mix in the lizards
> Mix in the lizards
> Stir and stir and
> Stir and stir and
>   Let's make a spell . . .
>
> And we will mix in the . . .

31 Monster stomp

John Per...

If you want to be a monster, now's your chance
'Cause everybody's doing the monster dance,
You just stamp your feet
Wave your arms around
Stretch 'em up, stretch 'em up
Then put them on the ground,
'Cause you're doing the monster stomp
That's right, you're doing the monster stomp.
    Ooh-Ah-Ooh-Ah-Ooh-Ah-Ooh-Ah
    Ooh-Ah-Ooh-Ah-Ooh-Ah-Ooh-Ah

Before you find somebody to chase
First of all you need a monster face,
You just show your teeth
Pull back your lips
Push up your eyelids with your fingertips
You just stamp your feet.
Wave your arms around
Stretch 'em up, stretch 'em up
Then put them on the ground,
'Cause you're doing the monster stomp
That's right, you're doing the monster stomp.
    Ooh-Ah-Ooh-Ah-Ooh-Ah-Ooh-Ah
    Ooh-Ah-Ooh-Ah-Ooh-Ah-Ooh-Ah

[Lyrics from score:]

stamp your feet | Wave your arms a-round | Stretch 'em up, stretch 'em up Then put them on the ground, 'Cause you're doing the mon-ster stomp That's right, you're doing the mon-ster stomp.

Grunt Growl Chorus (repeat as often as you like)

Ooh Ah Ooh Ah | Ooh Ah Ooh Ah

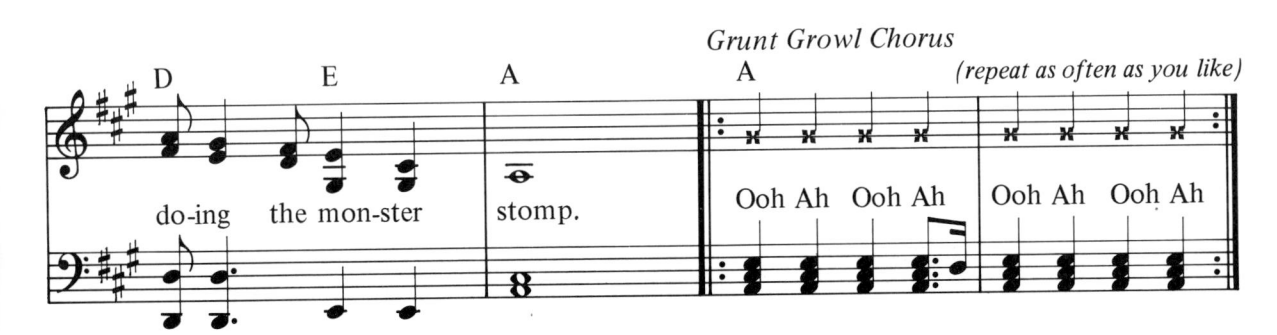

Basic use – an action song and dance

Sing it with everybody standing in a circle doing the actions. In the *Grunt Growl Chorus* the circle moves round with everybody pretending to be monsters.

Try this

☆ Repeat the first verse replacing "monster" with a different character each time – an elephant, Superman, and so on. Replace the line "you just stamp your feet" with an appropriate action for the character. Change the following lines also if you like.

☆ Children can paint pictures of their favourite monster or tell stories using the monster theme.

32 One two three

Leon Rosselson

One two three
Open your eyes and see
Sing it high and sing it low
For everyone and me.

The left must take the right
All around the ring
We've got to keep the circle moving
Everybody sing.

Basic use – an action song and dance

You can chant "one two three" until everybody is saying it together, then carry on with the song and all the actions indicated. At the beginning of the second verse make a circle, repeating the phrase "the left must take the right" until the circle is formed. Repeat each section as many times as you like.

Lively but not too fast

Try this

☆ In the second verse, break the circle and lead it to the centre in a spiral, getting gradually faster. Then go back to "one two three".

☆ Vary the song by singing it loudly or softly. Finish in a quiet way to bring down the level of excitement by singing "*sh – sh – sh*" to the tune.

☆ Think of other actions to fit into the song. Everyone could copy one person's actions, e.g. "Copy John, pat and pat your head", or "Be a dog, *woof woof woof woof*".

me. ____ The left must take the right All a-round the ring We've
sing. ____

got to keep the cir-cle mov-ing Eve-ry-bo-dy sing.

33 I've got a body

Harriet Powe

I've got a body,
A very busy body
And it goes everywhere with me.

And on that body
I've got a nose
And it goes everywhere with me.
And I sniff sniff here   (real sniffs!)
Sniff sniff there
Sniff sniff sniff sniff everywhere,
    I've got a body . . . *(chorus sung twice)*

And on that body
I've got some hands
And they go everywhere with me.
And I clap clap here
Clap clap there
Clap clap clap clap everywhere,
Sniff sniff here . . .
    I've got a body . . .

And on that body
I've got some feet
And they go everywhere with me.
And I stamp stamp here
Stamp stamp there
Stamp stamp stamp stamp everywhere,
Clap clap here . . .
Sniff sniff here . . .
    I've got a body . . .

And on that body
I've got some . . .

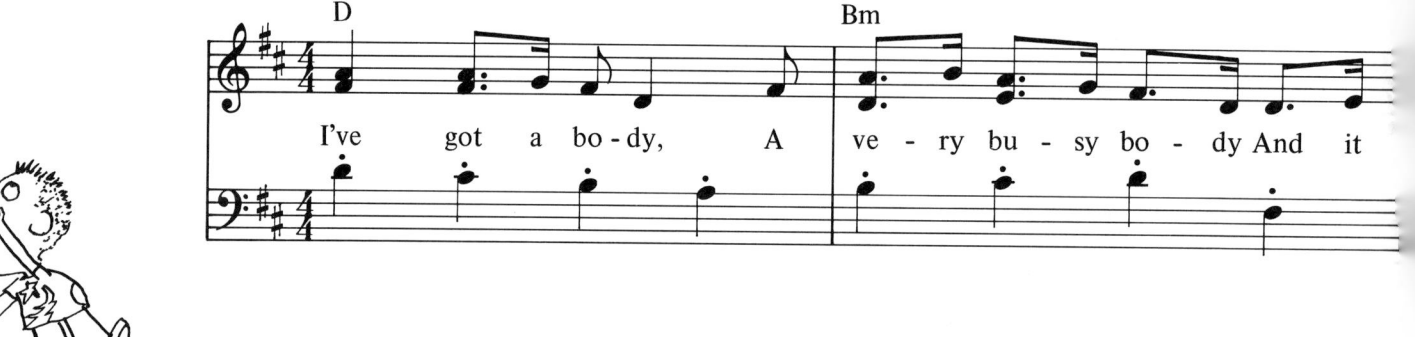

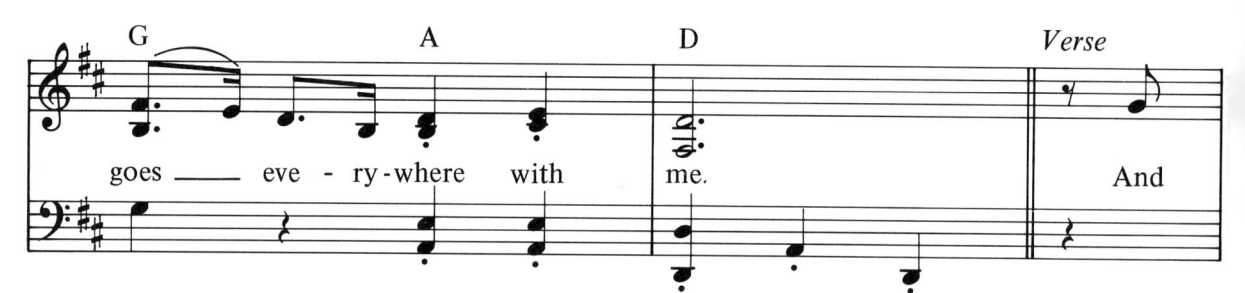

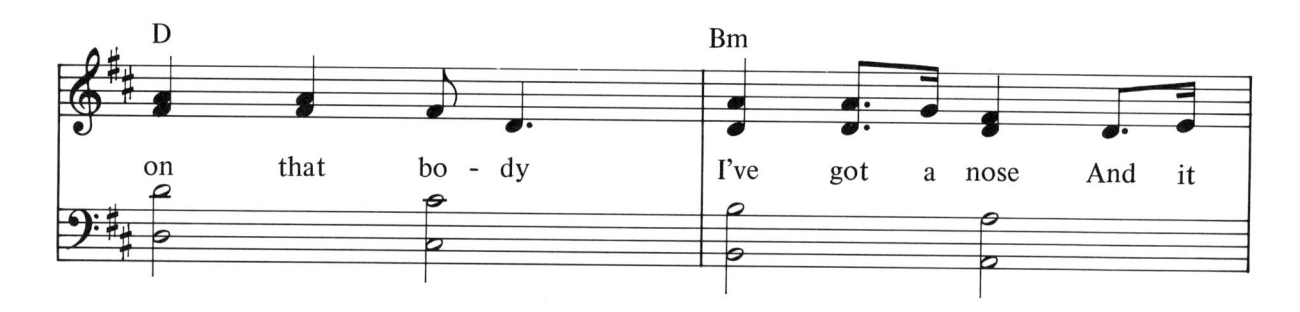

34 Drawing faces

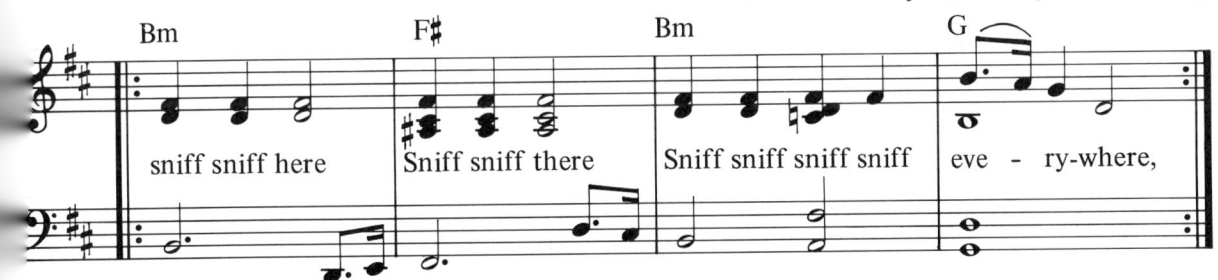

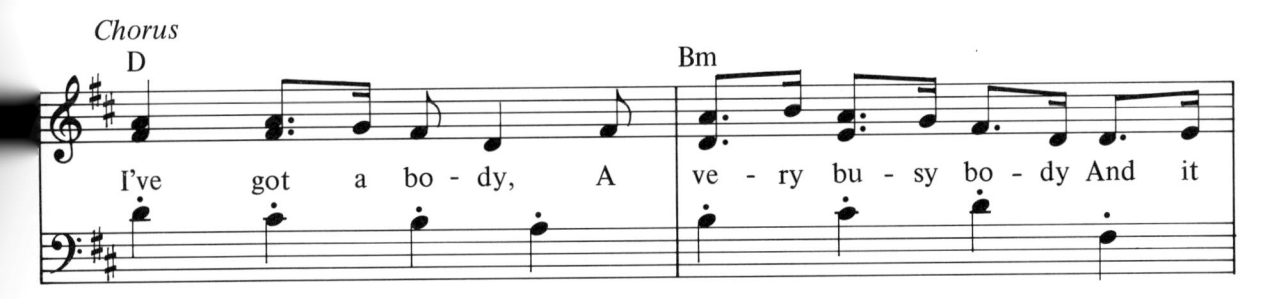

First time no repeat, then repeat as necessary

| Bm | F# | Bm | G |

sniff sniff here | Sniff sniff there | Sniff sniff sniff sniff | eve-ry-where,

Chorus

| D | | Bm |

I've got a bo-dy, A ve-ry bu-sy bo-dy And it

| G | A | D |

goes — eve-ry-where with me.

Basic use – a cumulative action song

Sing about different parts of the body each time, accumulating the actions as in the verses given here. When the children know the song, ask *them* to suggest a part of the body and what you can do with it. Use their suggestions as the basis for new verses.

- Each child chooses somebody else in the circle and draws their head and hair only.
- Then everyone swaps drawings and adds the eyes and eyebrows of their original child.
- They swap the drawings again and add the nose.
- Then they add the mouth.
- Everyone then votes who they think each picture looks like.

35 Mistletoe

John Pe...

Mistletoe mistletoe
Mistle mistle mistletoe
Adds to the Christmas cheer,
First you kiss somebody
And wish them a Happy New Year.

First you kiss your hand
Kisses are for free,
Turn round to a friend
And put the kiss on their knee.
    Mistletoe mistletoe . . .

First you kiss your hand
You've got a kiss to spare,
Turn round to a friend
And put the kiss on their hair.
    Mistletoe mistletoe . . .

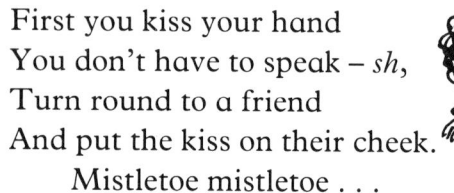

First you kiss your hand
You don't have to speak – *sh*,
Turn round to a friend
And put the kiss on their cheek.
    Mistletoe mistletoe . . .

Turn round to a friend And put the kiss on their knee.

Basic use – an action song for Christmas

If possible, sing the song while sitting under some mistletoe. Encourage the children to do the actions indicated, and to put their kisses on each other.

Try this

☆ Make up other verses for different places to put kisses. You may find some parts quite a challenge for a rhyme!

36 We can do anything

Pat Bar[...]

We can do anything
We can do anything
We can do anything
We want to.
   (Repeat)

We can sing this song
La lala lala,
Sing this song
La lala lala,
Sing this song
La lala lala la.
   We can do anything . . .

We can clap our hands
Clap clap-clap clap-clap *(real claps)*
Clap our hands
Clap clap-clap clap-clap,
Clap our hands
Clap clap-clap clap-clap clap.
   We can do anything . . .

We can whistle this tune
(Whistle the tune) . . .
   We can do anything . . .

We can . . .

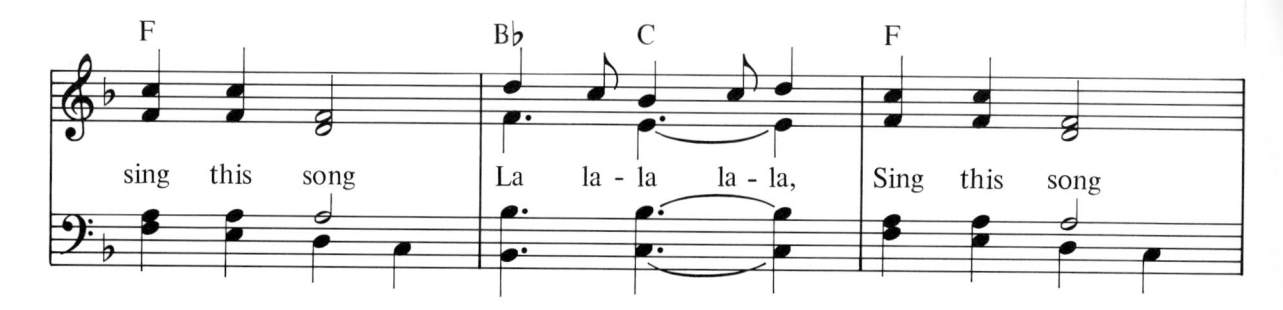

37 Ape

La la-la la-la, Sing this song La la-la la-la la.

Basic use – an action song

The verse is entirely adaptable. Do the actions suggested here or replace them with your own ideas.

Try this

☆ After singing the chorus, ask a child to think of an action for the others to copy. All do the actions while singing the new verse.

1. One child is the leader
2. And everybody copies
3. The leader tags someone else. "You're the leader now"
4.

38 Weather song

Harriet Powell and John Wesley-Barker

In all kinds of weather
Whether it's hot or cold,
Wouldn't it be nice if we could make
The weather do what it's told.

To make the sun
Let's all hum,
Hum hum hum
Hum hum hum.
   (*Repeat*)
      In all kinds of weather . . .

Too make the rain
Pat your knees,
Pat your knees
Pat your knees.
   (*Repeat*)
      In all kinds of weather . . .

To make the wind
Let's all blow,
Blow blow blow
Blow blow blow.
   (*Repeat*)
      In all kinds of weather . . .

To make the . . .

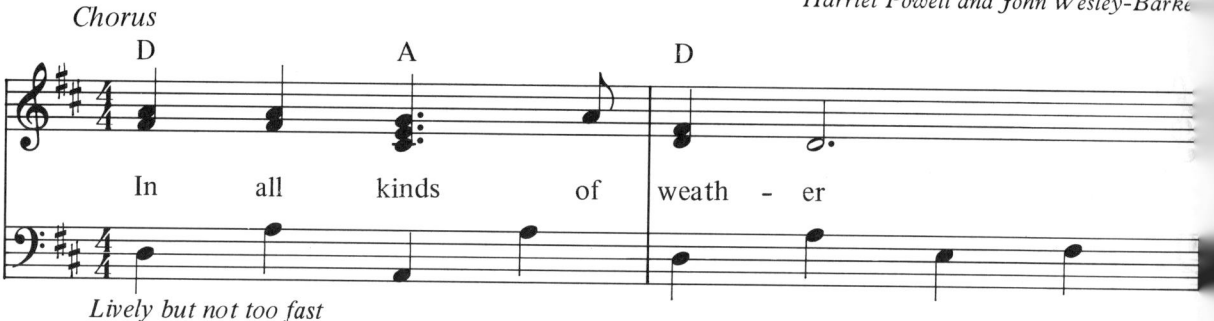

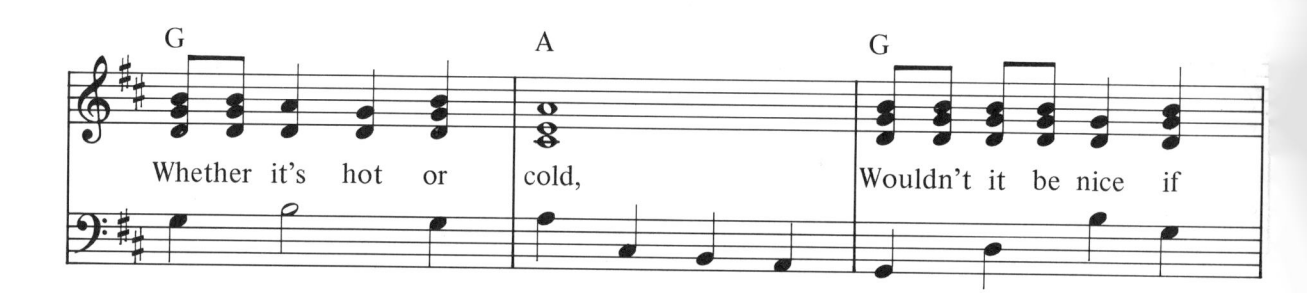

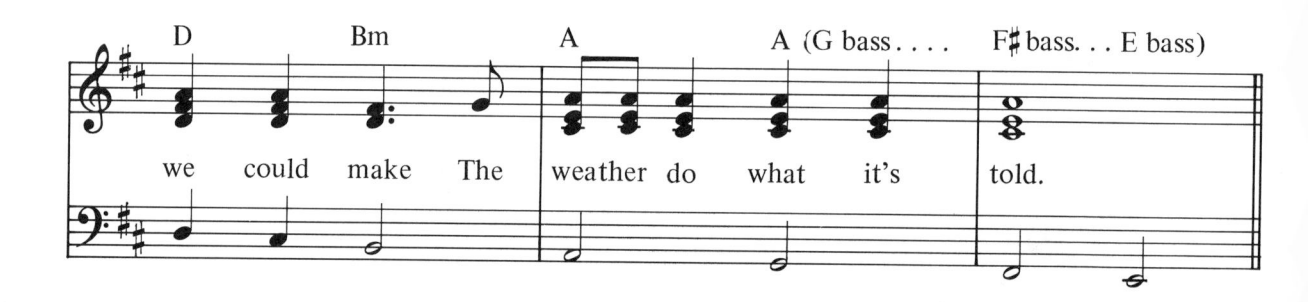

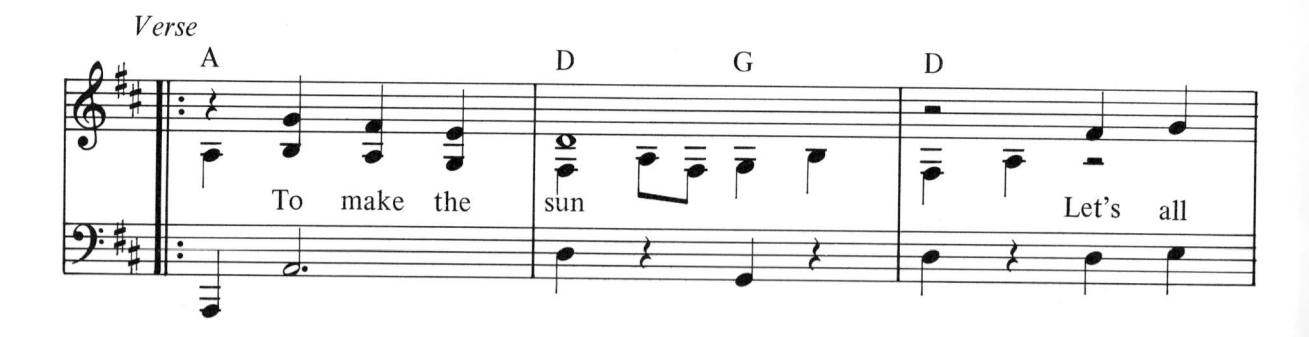

Lively but not too fast

Basic use – a sound and action song

After singing the chorus, take suggestions from the children for the type of weather they would like to make. Choose a sound or action to represent it. This could be the sound the weather makes, or the action or sound the children would make in that type of weather. You might pat your knees to represent the sound of the rain, shiver in the frost, and so on.

Try this

☆ Talk about the kinds of things you might *do* in different types of weather, make up a verse with appropriate words, and act it out, e.g.

> In the sun
> We go for a swim . . .

☆ Think about the clothes you wear for different weather, make up new verses, and act out putting on and taking off the clothes you need for each:

> In the snow
> Put on your boots . . .

> In the sun
> Take off your jumper . . .

39 Sound song

Harriet Pow...

Leader

Sounds we hear
Through the window
Far and near
Soft and still
High and low
Loud and clear

Children

Sounds we hear
Through the window
Far and near
Soft and still
High and low
Loud and clear

Together

Listen
Listen
Listen
Listen *(whispered)*

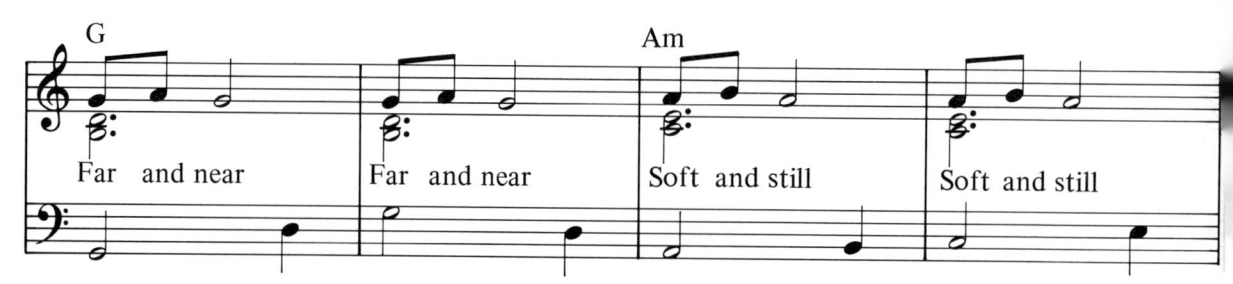

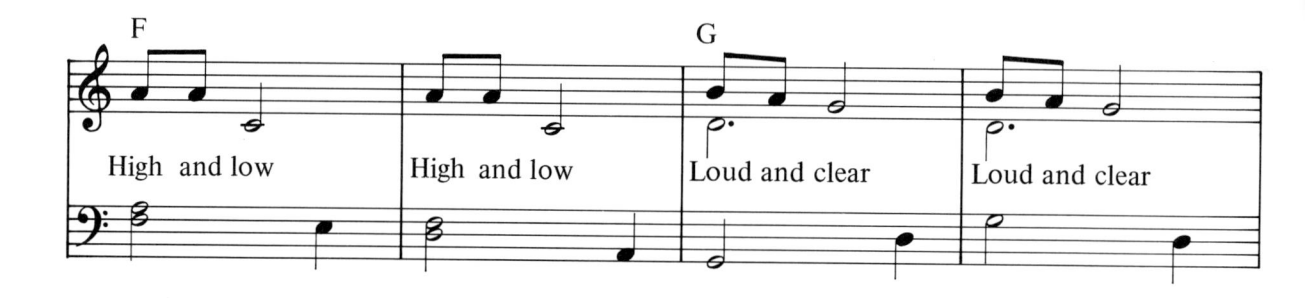

Slow and gentle

Sounds we hear / Sounds we hear / Through the win-dow / Through the win-dow

Far and near / Far and near / Soft and still / Soft and still

High and low / High and low / Loud and clear / Loud and clear

40 Storytelling

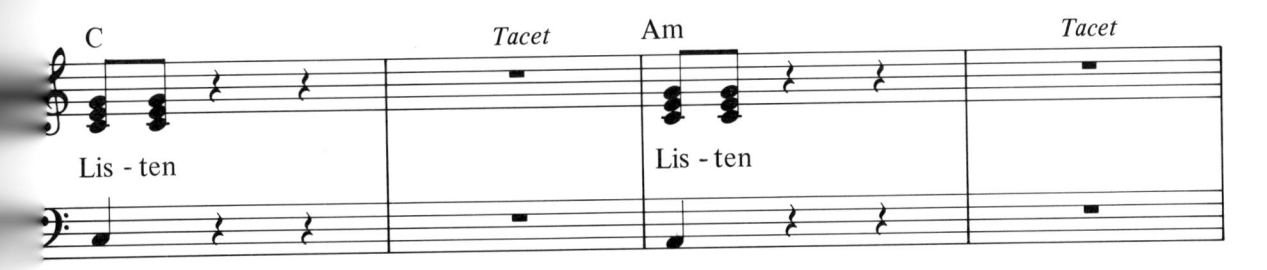

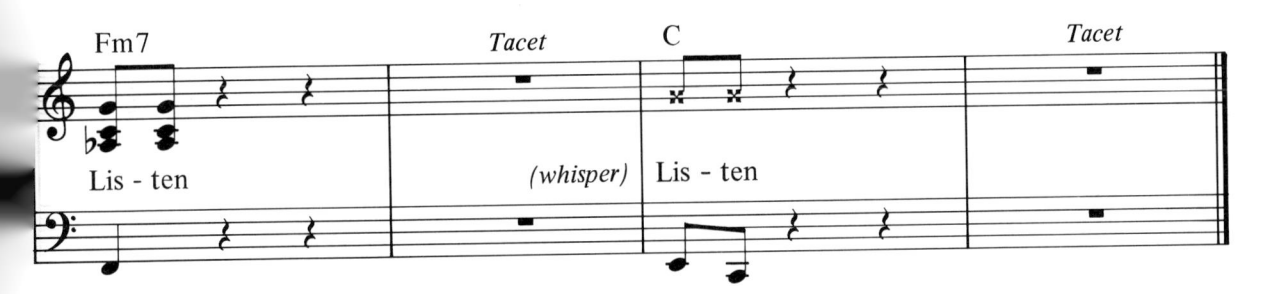

Basic use

This is a quiet listening song. The leader sings each phrase; the children echo it. After singing "listen", the children should stay very still in order to hear any sounds around them.

Try this

☆ Fill in the silent bars after "listen" with a sound for the children to identify. You could play an instrument hidden behind a screen, imitate bird calls – duck, chicken, owl – or record different sounds on cassette – keys rattling, water running, and so on.

☆ Choose a child to make the sounds for the others to identify.

1 The leader tells a story — "Can you add the noises to my story?"

2 Children add noises — "One day a robot walked down the road" — CLUNK! CLINK! CLINK! CLUNK!

3 "He sneezed" — Atishoo!

4 "Then he heard a bell ringing" — Ding! Dong! Ding! Dong!

41 Down on the farm

Judy Farrar, John Perry and Harriet Powell

Down on the farm
Down on the farm
Come and join us
It won't do you any harm.
   (Repeat)

You will see a hen
Sitting in a pen,
You will see a hen
Who's sitting in a pen.
   (Repeat)
Oh lay oh lay
Oh lay oh lay
Oh lay oh lay
Oh lay oh lay
    Down on the farm . . .

With a bit of luck
You will see a duck,
With a bit of luck
Then you will see a duck.
   (Repeat)
Quack quack quack quack
Quack quack quack quack
   (Repeat)
Oh lay oh lay
Oh lay oh lay
   (Repeat)
    Down on the farm . . .

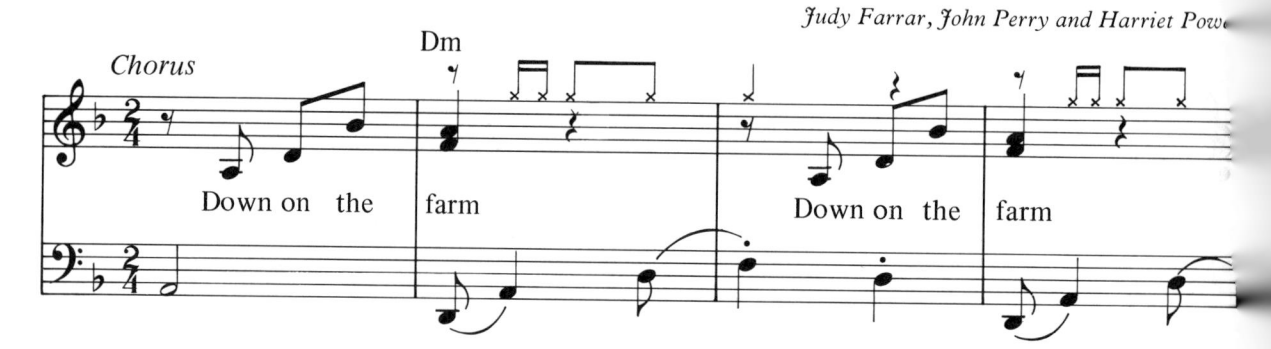

Inter-Action's City Farm in Kentish Town, London

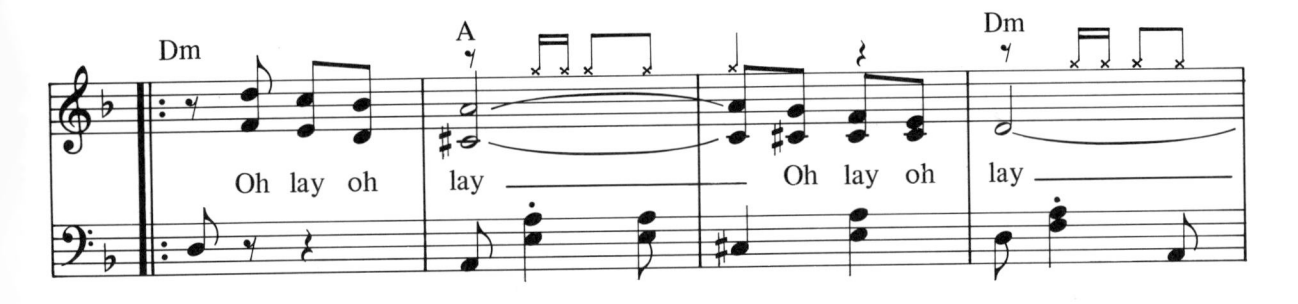

You will see a horse
Eating hay of course,
You will see a horse
Who's eating hay of course.
   (Repeat)

Munch munch munch munch
Munch munch munch munch
   (Repeat)
Quack quack quack quack . . .
Oh lay oh lay . . .
      Down on the farm . . .

You will see a . . .

Basic use – a cumulative sound song

Make the most of the Spanish rhythm by clapping, or using percussion instruments in the places suggested. Use the verses here and/or make up your own with the children, accumulating more sounds as you go along. The fifth and sixth lines of music can be used as an introduction to the song.

42 On Christmas Day

Harriet Powell and Peter Southcott

On Christmas Day hey hey hey hey
We'll have a tree hee hee hee hee,
And it will snow ho ho ho ho
For you and me hee hee hee hee.
   (Repeat)

He wants a car
He wants a car
And it'll go brm brm brm brm
Brm brm brm brm brm.
   (Repeat)
      On Christmas Day . . .

She wants a trumpet
She wants a trumpet
And it'll go toot toot toot toot
Toot toot toot toot toot,
He wants a car
He wants a car
And it'll go brm brm brm brm
Brm brm brm brm brm.
      On Christmas Day . . .

Basic use — a cumulative sound and action song

After singing the chorus, ask a child what he or she would like for Christmas and what noise the present might make. Make up verses using the answers, and inserting the child's name if you can, rather than the pronoun. Accumulate the presents and sounds as here.

43 Cumulative words

Verse

He wants a car _____ He wants a car _____ And it'-ll go brm brm brm brm brm brm brm brm brm _____ He wants a car _____ He wants a car _____ And it'll go brm brm brm brm brm brm brm brm brm.

First and second time no repeat, then repeat as necessary

1) On Christmas Day I will give my friend a lollipop

2) On Christmas Day I will give my friend a lollipop <u>and</u> a racing car

3) On Christmas Day I will give my friend a lollipop and a racing car <u>and</u> a ball

4) On Christmas Day I will give my friend a lollipop and a racing car and a ball <u>and</u> a furry animal

Try this

☆ Make up new verses by asking the children what they will eat on Christmas Day and what noise they will make while eating it. Verses can be made up about other Christmas day activities, what presents the children think they will *give*, and so on.

We'll all eat pudding
We'll all eat pudding
And we'll go yum yum yum yum
Yum yum yum yum yum,
She wants a trumpet . . .

44 Say goodbye

Maggie Anwell, Tony Coult, John Rust and Charlie Stafford

Leader	Children
Say goodbye	Goodbye
Say goodbye	Goodbye
Say goodbye	Goodbye
Say goodbye	Goodbye

Basic use – a ritual song for saying goodbye

Children sing "Goodbye" in response to the leader's "Say goodbye". Vary it by asking the children to shout or whisper "goodbye".

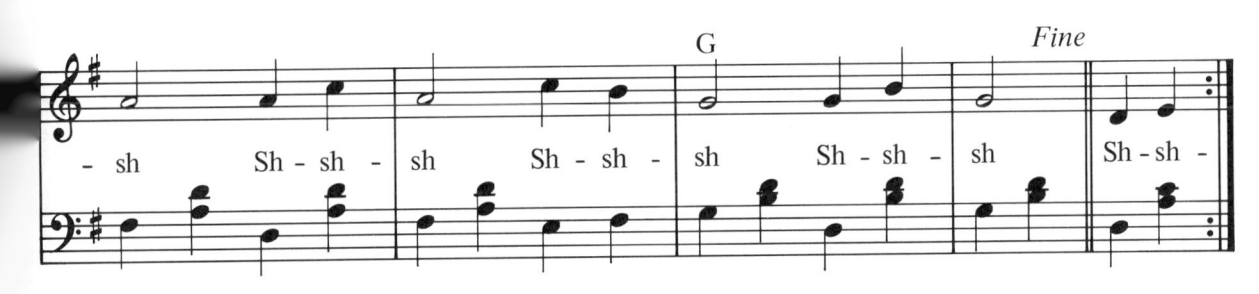

Try this

☆ Include the name of a child each time, singing one or two lines for each name:

> Goodbye Pete   Goodbye Pete
> Goodbye Pete   Goodbye Pete
> Goodbye Robert   Goodbye Robert
> Goodbye Robert   Goodbye Robert

☆ Fit in the words for actions:

> Give me a wave   (children wave) . . .

☆ If it is necessary to calm the children down, end the song in this quiet way (see above).

> *Sh – sh – sh*   *Sh – sh – sh*
> *Sh – sh – sh*   *Sh – sh – sh*
> *Sh – sh – sh*   *Sh – sh – sh*
> *Sh – sh – sh*   *Sh – sh – sh*

How the game-songs were developed

Prof Dogg's Troupe takes children's theatre to schools, playgroups, adventure playgrounds, festivals and theatres throughout the country. A variety of different projects has given rise to the game-songs in this collection.

Many of the game-songs were developed for use in shows. *How do you do?* was originally written as an introduction to the *Dolls Show*, which uses child-sized body puppets attached to the actors at the waist and feet. During a 20–30 minute play the dolls explore a theme set in domestic situations familiar to the children. Game-songs were written to explore the themes of colour (*Come to the party, Colour song*), sound (*Sound song*), numbers (*Dice song*), size (*Be a clown*), and Christmas (*Mistletoe*).

In the *Show Me How Show* for which *Keep on dancing, Walking through the jungle, Weather song* and *Make a face* were written, the children discover a clown puppet (one of Prof Dogg's Troupe) that cannot move, walk or talk. Gradually, during six weekly sessions, the children teach her all kinds of things from walking to talking, using games, acting-out, dancing and singing.

We're going to make a circus was originally a parade song for a street theatre show called *We're going to make a movie*. It was later adapted into a summer theatre project in which Prof Dogg's Troupe spend a day helping children prepare for and perform their own circus. Another street theatre show used *Monster Stomp* as its theme song leading the children into a monster-making project using junk materials.

Many game-songs were written for summer playschemes. *When a dinosaur's feeling hungry* was the theme song for a playscheme which involved children in building a massive junk sculpture of a dinosaur.

Other songs have been developed as frameworks for the type of participatory theatre which Prof Dogg's Troupe call an *Act-In*. This is a structure which involves children in dancing, playing games and acting-out characters, animals, etc, within an improvised story. The song links the different activities. Apart from the most obvious example, *Act in song*, many of the acting-out songs such as *Be a clown* and *Monster stomp* have been used in this way.

Prof Dogg's Troupe always provide entertainment at Inter-Action's *Festivals for Under-fives*. These events are presented twice a year, in the summer and at Christmas for playgroups, nurseries and anyone who works with under-fives in the local area. Each festival has a particular theme and setting, for example making toys at *The Father Christmas Factory* (for which *On Christmas Day* was written), the weather (*Weather song*), parts of the body (*I've got a body*), and shapes (*Bendy Toy*).

After all the excitement, Prof Dogg's Troupe find that the last song in the collection – *Say Goodbye* – is ideal for restoring calm. It can be sung quietly, fading gradually away to nothing with the repeated *sh sh*.

Show Me How Show

Acknowledgements

Dolls Show

Gathering together

The publishers wish to thank the following for permission to reproduce their work:

Pat Barlow for *36 We can do anything*; ED Berman for *2 How do you do*, *14 Act in song* and *21 Crying song*; George Dewey for *6 Come to the party*, *8 Make a face* and *25 Colour song*; Judy Farrar, Janice Honeyman and Katina Noble for the words and Harriet Powell for the music of *27 Keep on dancing*; Judy Farrar, John Perry and Harriet Powell for *41 Down on the farm*; John Perry for *31 Monster Stomp* and *35 Mistletoe*; Harriet Powell for *17 Be a clown*, *18 Walking through the jungle*, *24 Dice song*, *28 Bendy Toy*, *30 Make a cake*, *33 I've got a body*, and *39 Sound song*; Harriet Powell and Peter Southcott for *42 On Christmas Day*; Harriet Powell and John Wesley-Barker for *38 Weather song*. © Inter-Action Trust Ltd.

Maggie Anwell, Tony Coult, John Rust and Charlie Stafford for *1 Say hello* and *44 Say goodbye*; Keith Erskine for *12 Creep up*; Ian Heywood for *3 Bash and Bang Band*; Charlie Stafford and the children of Quarry Hill Flats, Leeds, for *10 When a dinosaur's feeling hungry*. © Interplay Community Theatre, Leeds.

Leon Rosselson for *5 We're going to make a circus* and *32 One two three*, © Leon Rosselson.

Every effort has been made to trace and acknowledge copyright owners. If any right has been omitted, the publishers offer their apologies and will rectify this in subsequent editions following notification.

We would also like to thank Carry Gorney and Liz Leyh for their work on the games; and Bob Chase and Alex Levac for their photographs.

Index of first lines

Be a clown, be a clown, 17
Bendy bends to any shape, 28

Come to the party come to the party, 6

Down on the farm, 41

His name is Pete, 22
How do you do? 2

If you want to be a monster, now's your chance, 31
If you want to be happy, 8
In all kinds of weather, 38
I've got a body/A very busy body, 33

Keep on dancing, keep on dancing, 27

La la lala la la, 14
Let's make a cake, 30

Mistletoe mistletoe/Mistle mistle mistletoe, 35

On Christmas day hey hey hey hey, 42
One two three/Open your eyes and see, 32

Sam creep up, creep up, 12
Say goodbye, goodbye, 44
Say hello, hello, 1
Sounds we hear, sounds we hear, 39

Take a little bit of yellow, 25
Tom, why are you crying? 21

Walking through the jungle, walking through the jungle, 18
We are the Circus Bash and Bang Band, 3
We can do anything, 36
We're going to make a circus, 5
We've got one dot on top of the dice, 24
When a dinosaur's feeling hungry, 10

Index of titles

Act in song, 14
Ape, 37

Bandleader, 4
Bash and Bang Band, 3
Be a clown, 17
Bendy toy, 28
Body patterns, 19
Burglar, 13

Clap clap game, 23
Clay modelling, 29
Colour collecting, 26
Colour song, 25
Come to the party, 6
Creep up, 12
Crying song, 21
Cumulative words, 43

Dice song, 24
Down on the farm, 41
Drawing faces, 34

Finger sword fighting, 16

How do you do? 2

I've got a body, 33

Keep on dancing, 27
Keep your face straight, 9
Knee boxing, 15

Magic statues, 20
Make a cake, 30
Make a face, 8
Mistletoe, 35
Monster stomp, 31
Musicless chairs, 7

On Christmas day, 42
One two three, 32

Rhyming name song, 22

Say goodbye, 44
Say hello, 1
Sound song, 39
Storytelling, 40

Walking through the jungle, 18
Weather song, 38
We can do anything, 36
We're going to make a circus, 5
When a dinosaur's feeling hungry, 10

Yummy corners, 11

(Game titles are given in italics)